Racial Discrimination

Comparative Discrimination Law

Volumes published in this Brill Research Perspective are listed at *brill.com/rpcd*

Racial Discrimination

By

Tanya Katerí Hernández

BRILL

LEIDEN | BOSTON

This paperback book edition is simultaneously published as issue 3.1 (2019) of *Comparative Discrimination Law*, DOI:10.1163/24522031-12340005.

Library of Congress Control Number: 2018967064

Typeface for the Latin, Greek, and Cyrillic scripts: "Brill". See and download: brill.com/brill-typeface.

ISBN 978-90-04-34594-2 (paperback)
ISBN 978-90-04-34595-9 (e-book)

This book is printed on acid-free paper and produced in a sustainable manner.

Contents

Racial Discrimination

Tanya Katerí Hernández
Fordham University School of Law
New York, USA
thernandez@law.fordham.edu

Abstract

This fifth volume in the Brill Research Perspectives in Comparative Discrimination Law surveys the field of comparative race discrimination law for the purpose of providing an introduction to the nature of comparing systems of discrimination and the transnational search for effective equality laws and policies. This volume includes the perspectives of racialized subjects (subalterns) in the examination of the reach of the laws on the ground. It engages a variety of legal and social science resources in order to compare systems across a number of contexts (such as the United States, Canada, France, South Africa, Brazil, Colombia, Peru, Hong Kong, Japan, Korea, Israel, India, and others). The goal is to analyze the strengths and weaknesses of various kinds of anti-discrimination legal devices to aid in the study of law reform efforts across the globe centered on racial equality.

Keywords

anti-discrimination law – comparative law – race – equality – discrimination – Critical Race Theory – subaltern – intersectionality – affirmative action

Part 1: Comparative Law's Resistance to Race

Racial discrimination is a topic rarely broached by comparative law scholars. While the reasons for this reticence as to addressing matters of race certainly vary across jurisdictions, a number of explanatory factors surface with greater frequency across a diversity of jurisdictions. To begin with, many modern scholars of comparative law were deeply affected by the World War II Nazi

 | DOI:10.1163/9789004345959_002

legacy.[1] The Nazi use of law to demarcate racial differences for genocidal ends led many comparative scholars to equate any legal examination of race with immediately racist purposes. Moreover, the Nazi reliance upon presumably "racial differences" across social groups to justify the enactment of racist laws of social and political exclusion[2] resulted in a reaction by modern comparative law scholars as to eschewing any use of law to specifically address race. In the shadow of the Nazi past, any overt legal acknowledgement of racial groups was in itself a racist action. For instance, comparatists Konrad Zweigert and Hein Kötz explicitly stated that their goal in comparative law was to avoid a focus on difference.[3] Race neutrality was preferred, accounting for the longstanding color blindness of constitutional equality provisions and any analyses of those provisions. The taboo status of racial specificity in law thereby discouraged many comparative law scholars from viewing racial discrimination as a topic worthy of study. Comparatists instead took a functional comparative law approach focusing on text-based analyses in the search for universal commonalities across linguistic translations. In short, the unspoken assumption was that the road to social and legal inclusion of diverse ethnic populations in any polity was by an insistence on fundamental sameness, with a concomitant trivialization or even denial of human diversity. Such comparative law scholars did not consider that an acknowledgement of diversity might be compatible with tolerance and inclusion.[4]

National Exceptionalism and the Denial of Racism

It is not only the long lingering shadow of the holocaust that has made comparative law traditionally resistant to engaging in an examination of racial discrimination. The comparatist exceptionalist notion that "true racial discrimination" exists in other jurisdictions, such as the United States or apartheid South Africa, has also been a contributing factor. Indeed, Eddie Bruce-Jones notes that although the Black population in Europe experiences racial discrimination, racism itself is understood as a U.S. relic.[5] With the advent of large-scale immigration from nonwhite countries, contemporary European scholars have continued to resist the salience of a race analysis in favor of

---

1 Vivian Grosswald Curran, Comparative Law: An Introduction (2002).

2 Amy Newman, The Nuremberg Laws: Institutionalized Anti-Semitism (Amy Newman ed., 1999).

3 Konrad Zweigert & Hein Kötz, An Introduction to Comparative Law 39 (in two volumes, Tony Weir, trans. 1977).

4 *Id.* at 11.

5 Eddie Bruce-Jones, Race in the Shadow of Law: State Violence in Contemporary Europe 26 (2017).

religious and cultural differences analyses. René Flores notes that European scholars generally agree that "though racial animosity may have been prevalent once, racism is not as significant in continental Europe as in the United States, and that cultural differences, especially religion, are the main drivers of anti-immigrant sentiment."[6] By way of example, Sweden removed the word "ras" from all of its domestic legislation, citing that race was based on an incorrect biological understanding of humanity.[7]

Yet, systematic surveys of immigrants themselves underscore the operation of racism. For instance, in Rene Flores's study of immigrants in Spain, it was found that the longer an immigrant's residence in Spain, the greater the odds of experiencing racial discrimination. However, this was only the case for non-European immigrants in contrast to European immigrants who instead indicated experiencing less racial discrimination the longer their residence in Spain.[8] The more assimilated the immigrant was with Spanish language fluency, the higher the odds of experiencing racial discrimination. Such data strongly suggests that racism is not a dynamic primarily driven by immigration status nor solely located in the United States.

Other regions have similarly engaged in a comparison to the United States that deflects from the salience of race in any region outside of the United States. For instance, Latin American racial denial has historically been facilitated by the deployment of strategic comparisons to the United States' racial regime meant to depict Latin America as innocent of perpetrating racism. I call this the rhetoric of "racial innocence."[9] As the Latin American human rights scholar Ariel Dulitzky has stated, "[a] kind of presumption of moral superiority *vis-à-vis* the United States of America is quite widespread throughout our region. Rarely does a conversation on this issue among Latin Americans take place without mentioning the serious incidence of racism and racial discrimination that exists in the land of our neighbors to the north."[10] For instance, in the 2005 BBC survey of Latin American racial attitudes, the following invocation of racial innocence was quite prevalent: "I don't think there

6 René D. Flores, *The Resurgence of Race in Spain: Perceptions of Discrimination Among Immigrants*, 94 SOCIAL FORCES 237, 238 (2015).

7 See for this legislative treatment of race in Sweden, LAURA CARLSON, BRP: COMPARATIVE DISCRIMINATION LAW: HISTORICAL AND THEORETICAL FRAMEWORKS (Brill 2017). pp. 99–100.

8 Flores, *supra* note 6 at 249–50.

9 TANYA KATERÍ HERNÁNDEZ, RACIAL SUBORDINATION IN LATIN AMERICA: THE ROLE OF THE STATE, CUSTOMARY LAW AND THE NEW CIVIL RIGHTS RESPONSE (2013).

10 Ariel E. Dulitzky, *A Region in Denial: Racial Discrimination and Racism in Latin America*, *in* NEITHER ENEMIES NOR FRIENDS: LATINOS, BLACKS, AFRO-LATINOS 39, 42–50 (Anani Dzidzienyo and Suzanne Oboler eds., 2005).

is much racism in [Latin] America because we are a mix of races of all kinds of Europeans, Africans, Asians, and other races that were or will be; but I understand that in many other parts there is racism, above all in the United States and Europe, is where there is the most racism."[11] In Suzanne Oboler's study of racism in contemporary Peru, she in fact found that as in most nations of the Americas, the U.S. laws of segregation constitute the ideological definition of racism.[12]

Indeed, Latin America has long prided itself on the historical absence of state-mandated Jim Crow racial segregation laws such as those that existed in the United States. When assessing contemporary racial conditions, Latin Americans continually make the comparison to the U.S. Jim Crow segregation history with statements such as "[t]here is no violent racism like in other parts of the world like neonazism or the segregation in the south of the United States."[13] "That is a problem of the Americans."[14] Conveniently, the use of the United States as a point of reference has long shielded from view the racial subordination of persons of African descent in Latin America. In fact, there is a region-wide phenomenon of denying the existence of racial discrimination because any "serious incidence of racism and racial discrimination" exists in the United States.[15] This observation is based upon an analysis of official nation state report responses to human rights violation claims before the United Nations Committee on the Elimination of Racial Discrimination. Despite evidence that racial discrimination permeates every realm in the regions of Latin America including social, political, education, labor, culture, and public health sectors, government responses downplay its significance as inconsequential compared to the legal violence in the U.S. context.

Country specific studies note that racial discrimination claims are treated as lacking merit because of the belief that Latin America is not a region with "real racism." For instance, Antonio Guimarães found in the Brazilian context that judges frequently dismiss claims based on the notion that Brazilian culture is immune from racial bias. Guimarães quotes one representative case in which the judge explicitly stated: "We do not have the rigorous and cruel racism

11 *Iberoamérica, ¿una región racista?*, BBC MUNDO (Oct. 13, 2005), http://news.bbc.co.uk/hi/spanish/latin_america/newsid_4331000/4331708.stm (hereinafter "Iberoamérica, ¿una región racista?").

12 Suzanne Oboler, *The Foreignness of Racism: Pride and Prejudice among Peru's Limenos in the 1990s*, in NEITHER ENEMIES NOR FRIENDS 75, 75–100 (Anani Dzidzienyo & Suzanne Oboler eds., 2005).

13 "Iberoamérica, ¿una región racista?" *supra* note 11.

14 Oboler, "The Foreignness of Racism," *supra* note 12, at 85.

15 Dulitzky, *supra* note 10 at 39.

observed in other countries, where non-'whites' are segregated, separated and do not have the same rights. That is racism".[16]

While not all judges are so explicit about how a particular comparison to the United States confines the recognition of racism in Latin America, other country-specific studies have observed a similar refusal to acknowledge the existence of racism in the enforcement of equality laws. For instance, in the examination by the Justice Studies Center of the Americas, of Colombia, the Dominican Republic and Peru, it was found that each of these countries suffered from a limited legal response to the issues of racial discrimination.[17] Similarly, Carlos de la Torre's inquiry into the Ecuadorian legal system discovered that the Ecuadorian government had a constrained view of racism as solely a problem of isolated verbal expressions of infrequent individual bigotry.[18]

Even within seeming court victories recognizing that racial discrimination exists, a problematic understanding of racism can be embedded. For instance in Jorge González Jácome's analysis of Colombian Constitutional Court case findings of discrimination, he concludes that the Court confines its understanding of racism to the acts of individuals with overtly manifested intent to discriminate in ways that problematically shields the operation of pervasive structural discrimination from consideration.[19] The focus on individual intent is yet another articulation of the vision of discrimination as exceptional in Latin American spaces.

Furthermore, the historical absence of official Jim Crow laws of segregation is used as a justification for resisting contemporary black social justice movement demands for racially conscious legal policies.[20] For example, when discussing the possibility of workplace affirmative action in Colombia, one commentator warns, "[t]hat would be like buying a ticket to a conflict we do

16 ANTONIO SERGIO GUIMARAES, PRECONCEITO E DISCRIMINACAO: QUEIXAS DE OFENSAS E TRATAMENTO DESIGUAL NOS NEGROS NO BRASIL 35 (1998).

17 JUDICIAL STUDIES CENTER OF THE AMERICAS, THE JUDICIAL SYSTEM AND RACISM AGAINST PEOPLE OF AFRICAN DESCENT: THE CASES OF BRAZIL, COLOMBIA, THE DOMINICAN REPUBLIC AND PERU (2004).

18 Carlos de la Torre, *Afro-Ecuadorian Responses to Racism: Between Citizenship and Corporatism, in* NEITHER ENEMIES NOR FRIENDS: LATINOS, BLACKS, AFRO-LATINOS (Anani Dzidzienyo & Suzanne Oboler eds., 2005).

19 Jorge González Jácome, *Esclavitud Perpetua: Constuyendo Una Perspectiva De Raza en el Derecho Constitucional Colombiano.* 55 VNIVERSITAS n. 111, 313–35 (2006).

20 Anani Dzidzienyo, *The Changing World of Brazilian Race Relations?, in* NEITHER ENEMIES NOR FRIENDS 137, 137–55 (Anani Dzidzienyo & Suzanne Oboler eds., 2005); Juliet Hooker, *Afro-Descendant Struggles for Collective Rights in Latin America, in* NEW SOCIAL MOVEMENTS IN THE AFRICAN DIASPORA: CHALLENGING GLOBAL APARTHEID, 279, 279–91 (Leith Mullings ed., 2009).

not recognize."[21] Another Colombian similarly states, "[i]f we do not want to create a racial conflict that does not exist in this country, we will have to lower the tone of the ethnic complaints and propose universal solutions, like the fight against poverty."[22] Similarly, the Brazilian reaction to the use of affirmative action in some universities is to denounce it as "the replacement of the Brazilian notion of racial democracy with a U.S. style positive discrimination that would generate polarization."[23] Indeed, a widely circulated statement of individuals opposing Brazilian affirmative action is entitled "We Are Not Racists: A Reaction to Those Who Want to Transform Us into a Bi-Color Nation."[24] It makes very little difference to such critics that affirmative action actually originated in India and not the United States. Such attitudes of racial innocence have also been reflected in the work of scholars comparing Brazil to the United States. For instance, Loïc Wacquant with his co-author Pierre Bourdieu, has been emphatic in asserting that the Brazilian racial context cannot be compared to the singular racism of the United States,[25] in much the same way that Brazilian anthropologist Yvonne Maggie has insisted.[26]

Yet Brazil and the rest of Latin America are not alone in presuming that racial discrimination is uniquely a U.S. phenomenon. Asian countries also deflect from their own racialized dynamics with the assumption that the traditional homogeneity of their countries has obviated any history of racial conflict necessitating the development of sophisticated discrimination legal structures and law. For instance, in Yujin Yi's examination of discrimination law in Japan and Korea, Yi concluded that both nations lack adequate legal frameworks to address racial discrimination despite very deeply rooted racist ideas of racial purity in each country.[27] While the national constitution in Japan does contain an equality provision that asserts that "All of the people are equal under the law and there shall be no discrimination in political, economic, or social relations because of race," Japanese courts have viewed the provision as

---

21 Catalina Gallo Rojas, *Igualdad Sin Cuotas*, El Tiempo, 7 (July 12, 2009).

22 Cesar Rodriguez Garavito, *En Defensa de las Acciones Afirmativas*, El Espectador (July 13, 2009), http://www.elespectador.com/columna150499-defensa-de-acciones-afirmativas.

23 Gonzalo Vega Sfrani, *Universidad Reserva La Mitad de sus Cupos Para Negros y Desata Polemica*, El Mercuiro, (Oct. 22, 2006), http://www.ifcs.ufrj.br/~observa/noticias/elmercurio/discriminacion_22.htm.

24 Ali Kamel, Nao Somos Racistas: Uma Reacao aos que Querem nos Transformar Numa Nacao Bicolor, (Sao Paulo: Nova Fronteira, 2006).

25 Pierre Bourdieu & Loic Wacquant, *Sobre as Artimanhas de Razao Imperialista, in* 1 Estudos Afro-Asiaticos 15, 15–33 (2002).

26 Divisões Perigosas: Políticas racias no Brasil Contemporâneo (Peter Fry et al., eds., 2007).

27 Yujin Yi, *The Status Quo of Racial Discrimination In Japan and the Republic of Korea, and the Need to Provide For Anti-Discrimination Laws*, 7 Colum. J. Race & L. 410 (2017).

applying only to those who are Japanese citizens or of Japanese nationality.[28] Moreover, because the courts also do not perceive the provision to be self-executing, the absence of a specific statute proscribing racial discrimination for all residents hinders the large number of Chinese and Korean nationals in Japan from having any protection from the racial discrimination they experience. Remarkably, even though United Nations human rights officials have repeatedly criticized Japan's lack of anti-discrimination law, the government of Japan has consistently argued that no such law is needed in Japan.[29] Debito Aruduo has noted that research on discrimination in Japan has similarly presumed that "foreigner discrimination" is not actual racial discrimination.[30] This lack of legal protection is compounded by the exclusionary force of Japanese immigration laws that grant citizenship based on whether an applicant's parents are ethnically Japanese, regardless of how long the applicant and the family have lived in Japan.[31] Even Japan's Supreme Court has acknowledged that a lack of Japanese citizenship necessarily leads to discriminatory treatment.[32]

Korea has a similarly structured immigration law that demands ties to ethnic Korean parents,[33] and a strong national belief that foreigners must be turned away in order for Korea to maintain its culture.[34] Nevertheless the Korean discrimination law covers both Korean citizens and foreign residents living within Korea.[35] However, Yi concludes that both the Korean and Japanese discrimination laws are weakly enforced because the bias against foreigners is normalized and understood as an immigration issue rather than a racial discrimination matter. This helps to explain why government officials are rarely held accountable for their acts of racial discrimination. A similar dynamic has also been observed in Hong Kong.[36]

---

28 NIHONKOKU KENPŌ [KENPŌ] [CONSTITUTION], art. 14, para. 1 (Japan).

29 DEBITO ARUDUO, EMBEDDED RACISM: JAPAN'S VISIBLE MINORITIES AND RACIAL DISCRIMINATION 3–4 (2015).

30 *Id.* at 28.

31 [The Nationality Law], Law No. 147 of 1950, as amended by Law No. 268 of 1952, Law No. 45 of 1984, Law No. 89 of 1993 and Law. No. 147 of 2004, Law No. 88 of 2008 (Japan) (http://www.moj.go.jp/ENGLISH/information/tnl-01.html).

32 ARUDUO, *supra* note 29, at 4.

33 [Nationality Act], Act. No. 8892, Mar. 14, 2008, *amended by* Act. No. 12421, Mar. 18, 2014, art. 5, (S. Kor.) (http://elaw.klri.re.kr/eng_service/lawView.do?hseq=32444&lang=ENG).

34 Yi, *supra* note 27, at 420.

35 [National Human Rights Commission Act], Act No. 6481, May 24, 2001, *amended by* Act. No. 11413, Mar. 21, 2012, ch. 1 art. 2, (S. Kor.) (http://elaw.klri.re.kr/eng_service/lawView.do?hseq=37724&lang=ENG).

36 Puja Kapai, *Status of Ethnic Minorities in Hong-Kong 1997–2014: The Rights of Ethnic Minorities Under The Law: Equality And Non-Discrimination*, UNIV. OF HONG-KONG: CENT. FOR COMP. AND PUB. LAW (2015).

Race as a Comparative Law Category of Study—Critical Race Theory

Over time, with the growth of human rights law internationally promoting the belief in the power of rights to correct social injustice, more comparative law scholars began to see race as a salient category of study.[37] The increasing global consensus regarding the need to explicitly prohibit discrimination has also expanded the number of jurisdictions to compare.[38] Crucially, with the advent of critical legal perspectives theorized by Critical Race Theory scholars, the color blindness of comparative law began to be questioned.

A new scholarly movement developed in U.S. legal academe in the mid-1980s, Critical Race Theory ("CRT"), in response to concerns regarding the inefficacy of civil rights laws to eviscerate racism in the face of conservative opposition and backlash to the civil rights movement gains. CRT questions the longstanding faith in liberalism and law to effectuate social change. Early advocates of CRT—including Derrick Bell, Mari Matsuda, Charles Lawrence, Richard Delgado, Kimberlé Crenshaw, and Patricia Williams—were all legal scholars from marginalized racial groups who challenged both the substance and style of conventional legal scholarship that discounted the voices and thus perspectives of subordinated social groups.[39]

The Voices of the Subaltern

Prioritizing the voices of the "subaltern" (populations that are socially and politically outside of the primary power structure of a jurisdiction[40]) yielded an alternative understanding of the role of race conscious legal analyses. Rather than being viewed as tantamount to an act of racism itself, race conscious legal analysis was instead seen as essential to appreciating the distinct racial positions that various social groups have *vis-a-vis* one another. Contrary to the traditional notion that racial subordination represents a deviation from the liberal legal ideal, this body of work recasts the role of law as historically central to and complicit in upholding racial hierarchy as well as other hierarchies of gender, class and sexual orientation. CRT thus focuses on studying and

---

37 Günther Frankenberg, Comparative Law as Critique 187 (2016).

38 Jean R. Sternlight, *In Search of the Best Procedure for Enforcing Employment Discrimination Laws: A Comparative Analysis*, 78 Tulane L. Rev. 1401 (2004).

39 Critical Race Theory: The Cutting Edge (Richard Delgado & Jean Stefancic eds., 3d ed. 2013).

40 Jean-Pierre Reed, *Theorist of Subaltern Subjectivity: Antonio Gramsci, Popular Beliefs, Political Passion, and Reciprocal Learning, Critical Sociology*, 39 Critical Sociology Issue 4, 561 561–91 (2012); Gayatri Chakravorty Spivak, *Can the Subaltern Speak?, in* Marxism and the Interpretation of Culture 271, 271–313 (Cary Nelson & Lawrence Grossberg eds., 1988); Boaventura de Sousa Santos, Toward a New Legal Common Sense 458–493 (William Twining & Christopher McCrudden eds., 2nd ed. 2002).

transforming the relationships among race, racism, and power with analyses that seek to reveal and challenge practices of subordination facilitated and permitted by legal discourses and legal institutions. CRT dares to look beyond the popular belief that getting rid of racism means simply getting rid of ignorance, or encouraging everyone to "get along" under a colorblind banner of social tolerance that overlooks systemic barriers to inclusion that are culturally normalized. One of CRT's most salient features is its call to context rather than universalism and abstract principles.

With the growth of CRT, contemporary comparative law scholars have begun to incorporate its insights for examining racial discrimination contexts beyond the United States. Adrien Katharine Wing's 2000 publication of "Global Critical Race Feminism: An International Reader" brought together many of the comparative law scholars deploying CRT into their work in innovative ways.[41] Thereafter, Mathias Möschel, assessed the benefits of directly incorporating a Critical Race Theory analysis into considerations of group conflict in Europe.[42] Furthermore, a helpful methodology for race conscious comparative analysis came to be articulated by Vivian Grosswald Curran.[43]

Cultural Immersion

Curran's "cultural immersion" approach overtly rejects the traditional comparative law premise that the analysis of racial difference in law itself is a racist endeavor. Cultural immersion calls for more than mere legal translation of a text. It instead requires a sociological inquiry to understand the subtext of a law and how it may be differently applied depending on one's racial position. For instance, most jurisdictions have equality law provisions inserted into their constitutions to assure equal treatment of its citizenry. Yet, it is a fact that not all social groups receive the same level of equal protection despite having constitutions that linguistically translate in similar ways. Indeed, economist William Darity, Jr. notes that economic disparity is correlated with race and ethnicity across a wide range of nations in ways that look remarkably similar.[44] For this reason, cultural immersion comparison requires an examination of political, historical, economic and linguistic differences that mold a legal

41 Global Critical Race Feminism: An International Reader (Adrien Katherine Wing ed., 2000).

42 Mathias Möschel, Critical Race Theory from the United States to Europe (2014).

43 Vivian Grosswald Curran, *Cultural Immersion, Difference and Categories in U.S. Comparative Law*, 46 Am. J. Comp. L. 43 (1998).

44 William Darity, Jr. & Jessica Gordon Nembhard, *Racial and Ethnic Economic Inequality: The International Record*, 90 Am. Econ. Rev. 308 (2000).

system and create cultural mentalities facilitating racial hierarchies. This is an expansion of the prism for comparison beyond simply legal texts. At the center of cultural immersion is the voice of the subaltern, providing a reality check for just how effective an equality provision or anti-discrimination law actually is.

The Efficacy of Equality Law

Searching for the voice of the subaltern is especially imperative within the context of comparative law, because not all populations benefit from equality law as much as others. For instance, Guy Mundlak has noted that in the case of Israel, some populations have a greater rate of success in advancing claims within the equal opportunities framework even though the equality law is neutral on its face and applicable for all citizens.[45] According to Mundlak, the Arab minority (Israeli citizens of Arab ancestry) is not positioned to benefit from equality law because of the negative effects of pre-market discrimination and their exclusion from key social networks of opportunity.[46] Pre-market discrimination includes the impoverished quality of education offered in the hyper-segregated spaces that the Arab minority is relegated to, and the poorly funded and weak infrastructures endemic to segregated Arab minority spaces.[47] Regardless of the fact that the Israeli Supreme Court ruled in 2006 that the government's method for allocating educational funding constituted illegal discrimination against its Arab citizens, the government has continued with its disparate allocations.[48] The adverse effects of the residential and educational segregation are further aggravated by the Arab exemption from the mandatory Israeli military service that provides significant social networking for future employment. Worse still, despite the fact that the law prohibits discrimination based on a person's military profile or duration of reserve service, many jobs require prior military or army reserve service and thereby exclude most of the Arab minority completely from consideration given their ambivalence about volunteering for a military known to enforce Arab segregation.[49]

Equality law then may exist on the books for all, but at the same time it can facilitate inequality and polarization as implementation of the law is embedded within the very biases and preferences that the law was created to address. For this reason, Mundlak warns that if anti-discrimination law is not attentive

45 Guy Mundlak, *The Law of Equal Opportunities in Employment: Between Equality and Polarization*, 30 COMP. LAB. L. & POL'Y J. 213 (2009).

46 Employment (Equal Opportunities) Law 5748–1988 (Isr.).

47 KATIE HESKET ET AL., THE INEQUALITY REPORT: THE PALESTINIAN ARAB MINORITY IN ISRAEL 11 (2011).

48 *Id.* at 23.

49 Michal Tamir, *The Freedom to Exclude: The Case of Israeli Society*, 49 ISR. L. REV. 237, 244 (2016).

to broader social frameworks of inequality, its outcomes will be built upon the same social cleavages, thereby resulting in outcomes that can polarize rather than equalize victimized populations entrenching the status quo. Hence the absence of substantive Israeli law prohibiting discrimination in housing effectively undermines the reach of the existing employment discrimination law to effectuate equality in the labor market. Nor is the absence of fair housing legislation a mere oversight. In 2012, a housing bill to prohibit discrimination in private housing was introduced and failed.[50] Rabbis have been public about urging Jewish citizens not to rent to non-Jewish Israeli citizens.[51] Arab citizens also receive unequal treatment in their ability to purchase or lease land and to obtain citizenship for their spouses.[52] Nor is Israel alone in how premarket discrimination hinders the efficacy of anti-discrimination law.[53]

Post-Race Assumptions

Moreover, other factors external to the text of anti-discrimination law can undermine the efficacy of anti-discrimination law. Another such external factor is the predisposition of judges to find allegations of racial discrimination non-credible or inherently questionable. For instance, in an empirical analysis of the rate of employment discrimination case dismissals by judges in the United States, it was found that racial discrimination cases have the highest rate of court dismissal as compared to other forms of discrimination.[54] Compared to race claims, gender based claims have the lowest rate of being dismissed. The disparity in dismissal of race-based claims is consistent year after year despite the fact that they represent the largest percentage of discrimination claims filed annually. The disregard for race-based claims within the contemporary U.S. judicial system can be understood as part of the judiciary's conviction that true racism is primarily a historic artifact.

With the dismantlement of visible Jim Crow segregation and the cessation in television film coverage of massive physical brutality against scores of African Americans, the reality of racism became more attenuated for those not directly affected by it. Formal access to education and the labor market for certain segments of communities of color also created an impression that the legacy of racism was behind us. Over time, many judges and juries

---

50 *Id.* at 248 n. 72.

51 *Id.* at 237–38.

52 Edmund Sanders, *New Israeli Laws Will Increase Discrimination Against Arabs, Critics Say*, L.A. TIMES, Mar. 24, 2011.

53 William Darity Jr. & Ashwini Deshpande, *Tracing the Divide: Intergroup Disparity across Countries*, 26(1) EASTERN ECON. J. 75 (2000).

54 ELLEN BERREY, ROBERT L. NELSON & LAURA BETH NIELSEN, RIGHTS ON TRIAL: HOW WORKPLACE DISCRIMINATION LAW PERPETUATES INEQUALITY (2017).

came to discrimination claims without the metaphorical glue of a conviction in the reality of racism. At the same time, the conservative majority of the Supreme Court employed what Ian Haney-López terms "intentional blindness" to purposely undercut the jurisprudential ability to locate triable claims of discrimination.[55]

Thus, at present even the most well-intentioned fact-finders can find themselves struggling to ferret out space in the anti-discrimination doctrine to make sense of the discrimination claims presented. It is not so much that the nature of discrimination has completely changed, but that the social norms for identifying discrimination have changed. Today the presumed "post-racial" social norm is that racism is an aberration instigated by consciously malicious individuals.[56] With that as the norm for identifying discrimination, fact-finders feel constrained from connecting racial disparity and an employer's flimsy or absent justification for the disparity with a finding of discrimination.[57] In this way, despite its historical and political differences from other nations, the United States shares the ubiquitous belief that "true racism" is rare, extreme and caused by atypical residents rather than a systemic-wide problem with subtle manifestations. This commonality will be evident in the examination of many of the legal systems that follow.

General Equality Principles

Before examining the particulars of anti-discrimination law across jurisdictions, it will be useful to introduce from the start the general equality principles that typically ground how to prove a claim of discrimination. Above all, the law understands discrimination as an unjustified difference in treatment informed by specifically prohibited considerations (such as race or gender) that causes harm. Not all human differences are protected by law from discrimination. For instance, some people may have more favorable views of tall as opposed to short persons, but anti-discrimination law does not cover height-bias. Courts

---

55 Ian Haney-López, "*Intentional Blindness*," 87 N.Y.U. L. REV. 1779, 1861 (2012) ("Intentional blindness, not intentional ignorance, more aptly characterizes the racial jurisprudence of the Supreme Court's conservatives. They seem to understand that racism is a pervasive problem, yet oppose the courts and the Constitution to contribute to the solution.").

56 Sumi Cho, *Post-Racialism*, 94 IOWA L. REV. 1589, 1597–98 (2009).

57 *E.g.*, Michael Selmi, *Theorizing Systemic Disparate Treatment Law: After* Wal-Mart v. Dukes, 32 BERKELEY J. EMP. & LAB. L. 477, 480–81, 492 (2011) (predicting that after *Dukes* courts will require a "narrative of discrimination" to justify a claim of systemic discrimination because of the modern absence of a presumption that statistical disparity is automatically explained as discrimination).

refer to those traits that are protected by law as "protected classes" or "protected groups."

Race is a protected category and a person of any race can bring a claim of discrimination. In examining whether a claimant has proven that discrimination occurred, a court conducts an inquiry into what was done and how the claimant was adversely treated because of their racial difference. To articulate a coherent claim, it is thus mandatory to overtly assert that race was the prohibited category that influenced the differential treatment. For that reason, it is necessary for the claimant to identify their race as the racial difference that motivated the ill treatment. However, this is not a litmus test of racial identity. It is a review of actions and their results. Racial identity is relevant only inasmuch as it illuminates how it motivated the adverse treatment. Hence, specific racial categories are not listed in the text of any anti-discrimination law nor do courts limit the law to particular racial groups. Moreover, the same standard of proof applies to all race discrimination claims regardless of what the claimant's racial identity is.

The text of many statutes and case law are in no way limited to a black-white understanding of race. Instead they allow for capacious ways of considering how harmful treatment was "on the ground of or because of race or color." For this reason, groups other than African Americans such as Asian Americans, Latinos/as and Native Americans are able to use the very same legal protections against discrimination as African Americans. The abstract and open-ended nature of the language of the laws means that judges have a central role in interpreting what discrimination means.[58]

Judges find that often the most persuasive articulation of racial discrimination is made when the claimant can specifically identity how persons of another race in similar circumstances were not exposed to the same adverse treatment as the claimant. Such a comparison to a similarly situated "comparator" not of the claimant's racial background is not required by law but is useful to courts in identifying the differential treatment. A similar analysis applies when women are compared to men in gender discrimination claims, or disabled persons are compared to able-bodied persons in disability discrimination claims. In short, anti-discrimination law inquires about race and racial categories because its concern is the prohibition against using race as a basis for harming people.

58 Kimberle Williams Crenshaw, *Race, Reform, and Retrenchment: Transformation and Legitimation in Antidiscrimination Law*, 101 HARVARD L. REV. 1331, 1331–1387, 1344 (1988) ("As expansive and restrictive views of antidiscrimination law reveal, there is simply no self-evident interpretation of civil rights inherent in the terms themselves.").

Tarunabh Khaitan explains that globally discrimination law maintains a divide between the public and private in which the legal duty not to discriminate is only imposed upon persons and institutions that interact with the public and are in a position to grant or deny access to goods or services.[59] Such public duty bearers include the state, employers, landlords, hotels, restaurants and other service providers. While private individuals may certainly harbor prejudices and even make decisions based upon those prejudices, the legal duty not to discriminate does not include them. Anti-discrimination law focuses upon public duty bearers because of their power as gatekeepers of opportunities, basic goods and social mobility. Private individuals acting outside of public spheres do not have the same potential for influencing societal opportunity. Khaitan provides the following example:

> [A] consumer who refuses to shop at a store simply because its proprietor is Muslim has probably not violated any law, even though most people would condemn such refusal as discriminatory. The law does not require us to refrain from discriminating on the ground of race in the choice of our friends either.[60]

This is why anti-discrimination law is unidirectional in nature. Employees are not prohibited against holding racial bias against their employers. Nor are tenants and consumers regulated in expressing racial bias however odious those expressions may be. The liberty right to hold bias along with a plethora of other perspectives and opinions is sustained until it materially encroaches on another's access to public goods. In other words, anti-discrimination law's primary concern is with public effects and not personal expressions of bias.

Considerations for Comparatists Working with Race

The particulars of what it means to do the work of a comparatist within the context of racial anti-discrimination law entails a number of considerations that legal scholar Hugo Rojas has usefully detailed.[61] Rojas recommends that at least eight different factors be compared beyond simply what the text of the laws provide. The Rojas checklist for unearthing what substantively constitutes

---

59 Tarunabh Khaitan, A Theory of Discrimination Law (2015).

60 *Id.* at 2.

61 Hugo Rojas, *Legal Responses to Discriminatory Actions: A Comparative Analysis*, 5 Loy. U. Chi. Int'l Rev. 127 (2008).

a discriminatory act and how various social groups are positioned to benefit or be disadvantaged by it, includes examining:

1) Is there a nondiscrimination principle in the national constitution? As interpreted by judges, does the constitutional equality principle permit benign race-conscious policies designed to mitigate racial disparities and barriers to inclusion?
2) Is international law incorporated into the domestic law such that positive action (affirmative action) is a permissible remedy?
3) What does the domestic law view as discrimination? Is proof of a subjective intent to discriminate required or are systemic disparities objective proof of discrimination?
4) What mechanisms are permitted for remedying discrimination?
5) Is the bulk of the discrimination law in the penal code thereby limiting remedies to administrative fees or jail sentencing?
6) Are compensatory damages permitted with civil law remedies or otherwise?
7) What is the role of the judiciary? Are trials limited to the submission of written briefs or can the parties speak for themselves in oral trials?
8) Do specialized agencies exist to enforce the law with consistency and vigor?

The benefit of the Rojas' checklist is that it encourages the comparison not only of the discrimination laws themselves but also whatever procedural differences can deter or encourage the filing of claims and effect the fullness of relief. The relevance of examining the procedural along with the substantive aspects of anti-discrimination law, is illustrated in the next part.

Part 2: Procedural Law Comparisons as to Equality Claims

The procedural structures and rules for presenting and processing claims of discrimination are as equally important as the content of a jurisdiction's substantive law. This is because differences in procedure can result in the inefficacy of even the most stellar of legal enactments. If a discrimination claim cannot be adequately enforced because of procedural devices that impose intractable obstacles for the parties, then the discrimination law has very little value regardless of what its text may articulate.

Jean Sternlight's assessment of employment discrimination procedures in Australia, Britain and the United States reveals that despite the growing global consensus about the need to legislate anti-discrimination laws, nothing approaching consensus has yet emerged regarding the best procedural method with which to litigate and resolve a claim.[62] Therefore, Sternlight's recommendation that a jurisdiction offer a variety of procedural devices, is viewed as particularly necessary in the context of discrimination law. Sternlight notes that across diverse jurisdictions, discrimination law entails a series of factors that raise distinctive private and public interests. Her list of ten factors include:

1) Laws prohibiting discrimination tend to be quite complex in their search for identifying nuanced social interactions with multiple motivations that are not always explicitly articulated
2) Facts pertinent to claims of discrimination are often highly contested and confusing
3) Disputes regarding discrimination tend to involve significant nonlegal as well as nonlegal interests
4) Society has a need for correct determinations
5) Society has a need for clear and public precedents to deter future wrongdoers and let persons know what conduct is permissible
6) Victims of discrimination must be adequately compensated
7) Many societies have a further interest in punishing wrongdoers
8) Alleged victims of discrimination must have adequate access to a procedural mechanism that allows them to assert their claims
9) Discrimination claims must be resolved quickly in order to permit all persons involved to get on with their lives and business
10) Alleged victims of discrimination tend to have fewer resources than do alleged perpetrators of discrimination

Jurisdictions are using a variety of procedural devices ranging from traditional litigation in ordinary courts, formal adversarial processes in specialized tribunals or before governmentally appointed arbitrators, privately imposed binding arbitration, nonbinding administrative or arbitral processes, and variations on mediation or conciliation.

Alternative Dispute Resolution

Arbitration is one of the ADR (alternative dispute resolution) methods addressed here. With arbitration, the disputing parties involved present their disagreement to one or a panel of private, independent and qualified third party "arbitrators." The arbitrator(s) determine the outcome of the case. While it may be less expensive and more accessible than formal court trials, the arbitration process has well-defined disadvantages. Some of these include the

62 Sternlight, *supra* note 38, at 1405.

loss of established rules of procedure and evidence, as well as the potential loss of control over the decision after transfer by the parties of decision-making authority to the arbitrator. By employing arbitration, the parties lose their ability to participate directly in the process. In addition, parties in arbitration are confined by traditional legal remedies that do not encompass creative, innovative, or forward-looking solutions to disputes.

Mediation is another ADR method where a neutral and impartial third party, the mediator, facilitates dialogue in a structured multi-stage process to help parties reach a conclusive and mutually satisfactory agreement. A mediator assists the parties in identifying and articulating their own interests, priorities, needs and wishes to each other. Mediation is a non-adversarial dispute resolution tool that is complementary to the existing court system and the practice of arbitration. If the parties do not arrive at any settlement agreement as a result of the mediation process, they are always allowed to go to arbitration or litigation; thus, mediation does not deprive parties of their right to due process.

Another important difference between arbitration and mediation exists in regards to choosing the neutral party. In choosing an arbitrator, the parties seek to select an individual that possesses particular legal skills, knowledge and competence. Both procedures are confidential as the parties allow a neutral third- party to discuss or decide the dispute without exposing the parties' dealings to public scrutiny or judgment. Specifically, the statements of a party during mediation are confidential and may not be disclosed without written consent. Generally, confidentiality in mediation also extends to documents specifically prepared for mediation, such as mediation briefs.

One unique feature of mediation is that any party, unilaterally, can decide to stop the mediation at any time if they believe the process is not productive, as opposed to an arbitration proceeding, which needs a common approval to discontinue. To be effective, mediation must be considered by the parties as a tool or instrument that the parties can use to manage directly the resolution of their disputes between one another. The focus is their direct, active participation as opposed to the increasingly detached role the parties play in an arbitration proceeding "run" by an arbitrator.

Conciliation, a third ADR alternative, is fundamentally different than mediation and arbitration in several respects. Conciliation is a method often employed in many civil law countries. For instance, in Italy it is more commonly used than mediation, particularly in labor and consumer disputes. The "conciliator" is an impartial person that assists the parties by driving their negotiations and directing them towards a satisfactory agreement. It is unlike arbitration in that conciliation is a much less adversarial proceeding; it seeks to identify a right that has been violated and searches to find the optimal solution. Conciliation tries to individualize the optimal solution and direct parties towards a satisfactory common agreement.

Although this sounds strikingly similar to mediation, there are important differences between the two methods of dispute resolution. In conciliation, the conciliator plays a relatively direct role in the actual resolution of a dispute and even advises the parties on certain solutions by making proposals for settlement. In conciliation, the conciliator is usually seen as an authority figure who is responsible for figuring out the best solution for the parties. The conciliator, not the parties, often develops and proposes the terms of settlement. The parties come to the conciliator seeking guidance and the parties make decisions about proposals made by conciliators. In this regard, the role of a conciliator is distinct from the role of a mediator. The mediator at all times maintains his or her neutrality and impartiality. A mediator does not focus only on traditional notions of fault and a mediator does not assume sole responsibility for generating solutions. Instead, a mediator works together with the parties as a partner to assist them in finding the best solution to further their interests. In addition, the role of the attorneys is different in mediation. Attorneys are more active in mediation in generating and developing innovative solutions for settlement. In conciliation, they generally offer advice and guidance to clients about proposals made by conciliators.

Conciliation is used almost preventively, as soon as a dispute or misunderstanding surfaces: a conciliator pushes to stop a substantial conflict from developing. Mediation is closer to arbitration in the respect that it "intervenes" in a substantial dispute that has already surfaced that is very difficult to resolve without "professional" assistance. The parties approach mediation as an alternative method to resolve their dispute, due to the fact that they both recognize that the conflict has grown potentially serious enough for litigation. Mediation may be used, however, any time after the emergence of a dispute, including the early stages.

Given the variety of advantages and disadvantages of these various procedural options for administering a discrimination claim, Sternlight concludes that it is desirable for a jurisdiction to offer multiple processes for resolving a claim. This is because some procedures primarily serve public interests while others primarily serve private interests. Specifically, the traditional litigation model serves the public interest by producing public judicial decisions that can provide guidance for how to construct a claim and its defense (and also be binding precedents in common law jurisdictions). In contrast, the private settlement procedures of mediation, conciliation and arbitration have no such transparency regarding prior decisions that can guide the public. Their benefits are rather in the faster time and lower cost that they provide the individual claimants.

However, the concern that mediation/conciliation can hinder the development of anti-discrimination jurisprudence is more than an abstract speculation. In a more recent examination of the Australian context, it was noted that only three percent of complaints are ever adjudicated. The vast majority are instead handled through the conciliation process without any public court opinions.[63] In 2014, only fourteen of the 443 complaints that were filed were adjudicated in court.[64] While parties do have the option to proceed to court if the conciliation process of the Australian Human Rights Commission is not satisfactory to either party, it is often the case that going through the conciliation process itself discourages complainants from going further. The time expended in the conciliation process wears complainants down and disinclines them from taking more time from their lives to begin a whole new court process particularly where court adjudications have been criticized for their narrow interpretation of what counts as discrimination.[65] Moreover, the Australian government's previous repeal of the anti-discrimination law that left its residents unprotected until it was reinstated some time later, has lead vulnerable communities to conclude that their position before formal law is precarious.[66] For this reason, Dylan Lino has asserted that anti-discrimination law should operate in conjunction with an explicit constitutional ban on discrimination that would hinder the legislature from repealing its statutory discrimination protections in the future.[67]

Burdens of Proof

The tremendous significance of comparing procedural aspects of discrimination law are particularly evident when comparing burdens of proof. A burden of proof is the obligation placed upon a party to prove or disprove a disputed fact. When the evidence proffered by the litigants is highly contested, it is

63 Simon Rice & Tim Soutphommasane, *The Racial Discrimination Act at 40*, 89 AUSTL. L.J. 303, 304 (2015).

64 Tim Soutphommasane, *Forty Years of the Racial Discrimination Act*, 40 ALTERNATIVE L.J. 153, 154 (2105).

65 Andrew Thackrah, *From Neutral to Drive—Australian Anti-Discrimination Law and Identity*, 33 ALTERNATIVE L.J. 31 (2008).

66 MICHAEL BANTON, THE INTERNATIONAL POLITICS OF RACE 88–97 (2002).

67 Dylan Lino, *Thinking Outside the Constitution on Indigenous Constitutional Recognition: Entrenching the Racial Discrimination Act*, 91 AUSTL. L.J. 381 (2017).

often the procedural burden of proof that will ultimately decide the case. Thus even where jurisdictions have similarly worded discrimination law statutes, identical fact patterns in those jurisdictions can yield very different results depending upon which party has been allocated the ultimate burden of proof.

Jarrett Haskovec notes that the differences in burden of proof in the United States as compared with the European Union are constructed to yield different results when litigants have presented equally persuasive evidence.[68] In the United States discrimination law workplace context, the burden of persuasion is always on the complainant-employee.[69] This means that if at the close of the evidence, the court cannot definitively decide which side has made the most persuasive case, the complaint-employee loses. Here, because the complainant-employee bears the burden of persuasion, he or she is said to thus bear the risk of non-persuasion.

In contrast, in the European Union's Race Directive it is for the respondent-employer to prove that there has been no breach of the principle of equal treatment.[70] Thus, unlike in the U.S., the EU Race Directive allocates a heavier burden on respondent-employers. The justification for the distinctive starting point for proving discrimination under the EU Race Directive, is that EU institutions wanted to make it easier for complainant-employees to establish a case of discrimination in order to root out discrimination more effectively.[71] In the more limited judge-led process of discovery that exists in most EU Member States, it is often difficult for a complainant-employee to establish sufficient facts to prove a case of discrimination because of lack of access to the documents in the employer's possession. The EU Race Directive burden of proof imposition on the employer attempts to blunt the effects of the disparity in access to evidence. In addition, the EU Race Directive mandates that companies keep records of their employment decisions. Therefore, despite the differences in legal systems between the United States and the European Union, comparing the respective burdens of proofs illuminates the challenges in enforcement that each system presents.

Examining a single fact pattern provides an instructive application of Haskovec's comparative analysis of the differing allocations of the burden of proof. For instance, consider a race-based variation of the hypothetical that Haskovec constructs as follows.

---

68 Jarrett Haskovec, *A Beast of Burden? The New EU Burden-of-Proof Arrangement in Cases of Employment Discrimination Compared to Existing U.S. Law*, 14 TRANSNAT'L L. & CONTEMP. PROBS. 1069 (2005).

69 St. Mary's Honor Center v. Hicks, 509 U.S. 502 (1993).

70 Council Directive 2000/43/EC, 2000 O.J. (L 180), art. 8(1).

71 Haskovec, *supra* note 68 at 1092.

> Unannounced, a white male supervisor enters the office of a black female employee named Ms. X, a highly qualified superintendent employed by the Postal Service Company for thirteen years. Ms. X, who recently put in an application for a promotion, suddenly becomes both anxious and excited, expecting that her supervisor has finally come to tell her the fate of her bid for a promotion. Before the superintendent has a chance to speak, the supervisor takes the initiative: "Ms. X, I have some bad news. You know the Postal Service Company is undergoing a massive reorganization. We're all forced to make cuts. Unfortunately, I had to choose to promote either you or Mr. Y [a white man], another superintendent and a capable man, and to demote the other. I had no choice but to pick Mr. Y for a promotion and you for a demotion. Mr. Y has more skill and experience in dealing with and supervising a large number of subordinates than you have, he has the ability to get the respect of his subordinates—an ability that is necessary for such a position of leadership—and he knows more about building services and maintenance. It was a tough decision, Ms. X, but I had to make it. I am sorry." With that, the employer exits the office.
>
> Ms. X strongly suspects that her supervisor did not actually choose to demote her for a lack of any skill or experience with people vis-à-vis Mr. Y; rather, she has substantial reason to believe that her employer decided to demote her because she is a black woman and not "a capable white man," who, seemingly by virtue of the fact he is a white man, has the necessary "ability to get the respect of his subordinates." Ms. X has had an outstanding history of performance at the Postal Service Company, always receiving "very good" or "good" evaluations in all skill areas, including employee relations. She received promotions and commendations frequently. Furthermore, Ms. X has had experience supervising forty-five to fifty people in her role as superintendent, while Mr. Y has supervised only fifteen people on a regular basis, and in her experience, most of Mr. Y's subordinates seem to grouse about him openly. Despite her strong credentials and experience, which she believes are likely stronger and more extensive than those of Mr. Y, her supervisor picked her for demotion and decided to promote the white male superintendent.[72]

With such a scenario, the U.S. allocation of the burden of persuasion on Ms. X, means she is unlikely to succeed when she has no evidence of the Supervisor's verbal or written admission regarding an intent to discriminate. In contrast, the EU allocation of the burden of persuasion on the employer means that

72 *Id.* at 1070.

unless the employer can provide concrete evidence that denying a promotion to a highly qualified employee and demoting her in favor of a less qualified person of a different race, was done with a legitimate business reason in mind, the lack of a legitimate justification will result in the employer failing to carry the burden of proof and the employee being successful in seeking a remedy for unlawful discrimination.

The contrast between the U.S. race law and that of the EU Race Directive, is especially significant when one considers that with the 2000 issuance of the EU Race Equality Directive, many more nations have enacted anti-discrimination legislation than ever before in Europe.[73] Under the Race Directive, EU Member States are required to prohibit discrimination on the grounds of race or ethnic origin. For some Member States this has meant the introduction, for the first time of the adoption of a range of measures and a legal architecture for individuals to pursue their rights. These include Bulgaria, Cyprus, Estonia, Lithuania, Hungary, Poland, Romania, the Slovak Republic, Slovenia, and Spain. The EU mandate provides a higher level of protection for racialized groups in Member States.

Nevertheless, there are still differences across the national frameworks that leave racialized groups vulnerable. The EU Commission itself has noted that most EU members do not correctly apply the burden of proof, thereby undermining the full potential of the legal reform.[74] For instance, Busstra describes Estonia law as providing for an overly broad justification for discrimination that thus makes the law ineffective against discrimination.[75] Busstra theorizes that the Race Directive was not favorably received in Estonia as discrimination was perceived to be a non-issue within a cultural context that assumes individual effort and not systemic bias is the cause of a person's fortune and accusations of discrimination are inappropriate excuses for individual failure. In short, what all the aforementioned examples indicate is that procedural devices for how to administer a discrimination claim carry significant consequences for how expansively or narrowly anti-discrimination law is enforced. Similarly, the definition of what is racial discrimination is just as significant and is therefore discussed in the next part.

---

73 M.J. Busstra, The Implications of the Racial Equality Directive for Minority Protection within the European Union (2011).

74 Lilla Farkas & Orlagh O'Farrell, EU Commission, Reversing the Burden of Proof: Practical Dilemmas at the European and National Level 60, 60–70 (2014).

75 *Id.*

Part 3: Definitions of Discrimination, Equality and Race Discrimination

Conceptualizations of what is encompassed in the notion of discrimination are shaped not only by what the text of a law is, but also by the cultural context that interprets the text. Thus even jurisdictions with similarly worded legislation will not necessarily label the same range of actions as discriminatory. For instance, the Portuguese Constitution is expansive in its prohibition against racial discrimination in the contexts of employment, education and its ban on the formation of racist organizations.[76] Moreover, additional legislative enactments not only elaborate on the equality rights for the workplace,[77] and school contexts,[78] they also prohibit discrimination in the allocation of social and health protections; social benefits; and access to public services including housing.[79] Equality law is even specifically extended to the protection of the dignity of immigrants in relation to their nationality or ethnic origin.[80]

Yet, in a study of hundreds of discrimination claims brought before the Commission on Equality and Against Racial Discrimination during a seven-year period, only 149 were processed and of those only 7 had successful resolutions for the claimant.[81] The monitoring agencies in Portugal are critiqued for their conviction that true racism is external to its cordial culture[82] and thus their denial of racism when working with denunciations of discrimination.[83]

---

76 Constituição da República Portuguesa, VII Revisão Constitucional (2005) Artigos 13, 46, 59 & 69, http://www.parlamento.pt/Legislacao/PAGINAS/CONSTITUICAOREPUBLICAPORTUGUESA.ASPX.

77 Lei n.º 7/2009, Diário da República—1.ª série-N.º 30, 933 (2009) (Portugal) https://dre.pt/application/dir/pdf1sdip/2009/02/03000/0092601029.pdf (this provision pertains to Article 24 of the Labor Code, contained in the Annex of Lei n.º 7/2009).

78 Lei n.º 134/99, Diário da República—I Série-A, 5945 (1999) (Portugal) https://dre.pt/application/file/a/532477.

79 Lei n.º 18/2004, Diário da República—I Série-A, Artigo 2º [Article 2], 2971 (2004) (Portugal) https://dre.pt/application/dir/pdfisdip/2004/05/110A00/29712974.pdf.

80 Lei n.º 27/2005, Diário da República—I Série-A, Artigo 2º [Article 2], 874 (2005) (Portugal) https://dre.pt/application/conteudo/618939.

81 Ceu Neves, *Comissão contra a discriminação racial atua desde 2005 e apenas conseguiu sete condenações*, DIARIO DE NOTICIAS (Mar. 22, 2012), https://advance.lexis.com/api/permalink/9f08b576-3086-4e29-b491-5cbfb299e4f5/?context=1000516.

82 Ana Rita Alves, *Realojar, despejar, guetizar. Arqueologias de uma violência obliterada: habitação e racismo nos relatórios nacionais/internacionais*, CENTRO DE ESTUDOS SOCIAIS DA UNIVERSIDADE DE COIMBRA (Mar. 2018), http:/saladeimprensa.ces.uc.pt/?col=opiniao&id=16391#.W3bsUuhKjIV.

83 Silvia Rodriguez Maeso, *'Civilising' the Roma/Gypsies. Public policies, 'employability' and the depoliticisation of (anti-'employability' and the depoliticisation of (anti-) racism in Portugal*, 22 IDENTITIES GLOBAL STUD. CULTURE POWER 53 (2014).

With the "institutionalization of racism through a regime of denial,"[84] the presumption that claims of racial exclusion are caused by the cultural deficiencies of non-assimilated ethnic minorities like Afro-descended populations and Roma communities, rather than by discriminatory bias, cause the institutional misrecognition of racism.[85] This is the case, even when school children experience outright racial harassment and racist verbal abuse, school officials reinterpret the incidents as cultural misunderstandings and thereby interfere with the enforcement of anti-discrimination law.[86] Similarly, the racial exclusion that is rampant in residential segregation patterns[87] and is ubiquitous across schools caused in part from what Marta Araujo describes as "white flight," are both ignored in the enforcement of anti-discrimination laws.[88]

The Concept of Equality

In contrast, the expansiveness of the definition of equality and its antithesis of discrimination in other jurisdictions is greatly influenced by how central the concept of equality is to the formation of the constitution. For example, commentators have noted that the post-apartheid South African constitution was a socially transformative document with a new foundation for the birth of its multiracial democracy embedding racial equality as its core value.[89] As a consequence, South Africa's "substantive equality" approach to questions of racial discrimination is notable for its rejection of the traditional formal approach to rigidly insisting upon identical treatment for all persons as the goal of equality. Instead, South Africa embraces a contextual and asymmetrical analysis that begins with a recognition that the equality guarantee must be interpreted in light of past and continuing patterns of disadvantage. Thus, the constitutional

---

84 *Id.*

85 Araujo, Marta & Silvia Rodriguez Maeso, *The 'prudent' integration of Roma/Gypsy pupils: segregation and white flight in Portuguese compulsory schooling*, 19 J. Race Enthnicity & Educ. Issue 2, 300 (2014).

86 Marta Araujo, *O silencio do racismo em Portugal: o caso do abuso verbal racista na escola*, *in* Um Olhar Além das Fronteiras: Educação E Relações Raciais 77, 77–94 (Nilma Lino Gomes ed. 2007).

87 Ana Rita Alves, *(PRÉ) TEXTOS E CONTEXTOS: Media, Periferia e Racialização*, Revista de Ciencias Sociais—Politica & Trabalho, n. 44, 91–107 (Jan/June 2016), http://www.periodicos.ufpb.br/index.php/politicaetrabalho/article/view/28632/16531.

88 Marta Araujo, *A Very 'Prudent Integration': White Flight, School Segregation and the Depoliticization of (Anti)Racism*, 19 Race Ethnicity & Educ. 300 (n. 2), 300–323 (2016).

89 Christina Lee, *Toward a Transformative Equality: A Comparison of South Africa's and the United States' Constitutional Equality Doctrines*, 16 Scholar: St. Mary's L. Rev. & Soc. Just. 749, 769 (2014).

text mandate that "no person be *unfairly* discriminated against," thereby recognizes that some discrimination is fair.[90] Sara Jagwanth notes that:

> An important element of the substantive equality model—which is of importance to addressing previous disadvantage—is its asymmetrical application. Under an asymmetrical model, not all differentiation on the listed or unlisted grounds are equally problematic. Using this approach, it matters whether the discrimination being complained of is designed to remedy the wrongs of the past or whether it is designed to perpetuate an existing position of privilege. In this regard, a complaint of discrimination against, for example, black people or women will be qualitatively different from a complaint of discrimination against white people or men. This does not suggest that these groups can never be discriminated against, but it recognises that they do not suffer from structural disadvantage and patterns of discrimination on the basis of race and gender.[91]

For this reason, the South African Constitutional Court has stated that a racial classification "which is unfair in one context may not necessarily be unfair in a different context"[92] in order to eradicate past patterns of disadvantage. In short, while many other formal equality jurisdictions treat an allegation of discrimination as a search for whether there has been dissimilar treatment between groups of people, South Africa instead examines the discriminatory impact within the social and historical context it occurs. This imbues the South African constitutional equality guarantee with a remedial and restitutionary dimension that is rare.

Indeed, in Frank Michelman's comparison between South Africa and the United States, he observes that the differences between the constitutional antidiscrimination law of the two nations are quite striking because the United States (like many other nations) has over time developed an aversion to the idea of defining and classifying citizens on the basis of their skin color or racial group membership.[93] Michelman reasons that partaking in the construction of a new democracy after apartheid makes South African jurists "fully invested

---

90 S. Afr. Const., 1996 § 8(2).

91 Sara Jagwanth, *Affirmative Action in A Transformative Context: The South African Experience*, 36 Conn. L. Rev. 725, 728 (2004).

92 President of the Republic of South Africa and Another v. Hugo (1997) (6) BCLR 708 (CC) (S. Afr.).

93 Frank J. Michelman, *Reasonable Umbrage: Race and Constitutional Antidiscrimination Law in the United States and South Africa*, 117 Harv. L. Rev. 1378 (2004).

in the long-range commitments of their country's constitution that they do not feel maltreated—and so they are not maltreated (fusion being thus double-edged)—by government classifications fitted to the advancement of those commitments."[94] In application, the distinction between formalistic equality and substantive equality means that a race-based affirmative action program will often be treated as an act of discrimination itself in the United States (with the breach of identical treatment), whereas in South Africa affirmative action policies are often deemed "fair" discrimination for dismantling structures and practices of inequality. Darcy Du Toit also observes a similar dichotomy in the approach of the European Court of Justice (ECJ) as compared with the South Africa Constitutional Court, inasmuch as the ECJ emphasizes the right to equality as an individual right while South Africa prioritizes the need for corrective measures at the societal level.[95] More details about the South African approach to affirmative action will be explored in part 6.

Yet, it should be noted that substantive equality is not solely the purview of a jurisdiction like that of South Africa's, in which large scale law reform followed a social revolution like the dismantlement of apartheid. Canada never officially imposed a system of apartheid, but in its drafting of the Canadian Charter of Rights and Freedoms of 1982, it embraced a substantive equality approach in its concern with contexts of disadvantage and not solely formal symmetrical equality. This is because the Charter was crafted in consultation with independent advisory groups of racial minorities and others to give them a voice in shaping the legal framework.[96] As consequence, while section 15(1) of the Charter articulates the globally familiar edict that "every individual is equal before and under the law and has the right to the equal protection and equal benefit of the law without discrimination and in particular, without discrimination based on race," section 15(2) goes on to note that "subsection (1) does not preclude any law, program or activity that has as its object the amelioration of conditions of disadvantaged individuals or groups including those that are disadvantaged because of race."[97]

Bruce Porter notes that as conceived, Section 15 moved the protection of equality beyond a right to freedom from discrimination to a broadly framed

94 *Id.* at 1380.

95 Darcy du Toit, *"Affirmative Action" or "Positive Action" in the Employment Context: Comparing the Interpretation of "Equality" by the European Court of Justice with that of the South African Constitutional Court*, 36 COMP. LAB. L. & POLY J. 423 (2015).

96 Jessica Eisen, *Grounding Equality in Social Relations: Suspect Classification, Analogous Grounds and Relational Theory*, 42 QUEEN'S L.J. 41 (2017).

97 Canadian Charter of Rights and Freedoms, Part I of the Constitution Act, 1982, *being* Schedule B to the Canada Act, 1982, c 11 (UK).

guarantee of equality as a positive social right.[98] Section 15 was thus understood by equality-seekers to impose obligations on government to take positive measures to address systemic patterns of socio-economic disadvantage and to incorporate social and economic rights which Canada had affirmed under international law such as the right to housing, to education, adequate income and fulfilling work. However, Porter concludes that these central expectations have remained largely unrealized. Hart Schwartz similarly theorizes that the Charter equality rights have not been fully realized because of the return to a more formal equality focus on narrowing anti-discrimination law to instances when "similarly-situated" persons have not been treated identically.[99] Yet both Schwartz and Jessica Eisen note that there is also Supreme Court of Canada jurisprudence that shows a continued commitment to substantive equality.[100]

Lolita Buckner Inniss agrees with the unrealized potential of the Charter, particularly with respect to the equality expectations of blacks in Canada.[101] Inniss notes that while anti-racism is enshrined in the law and culture of the nation, blacks in Canada remain outsiders without full acceptance in what defines civil membership. She attributes this to the cultural misguided belief that racial classifications are themselves the source of historic and ongoing anti-black discrimination. As a result, the national preference for combating racism is by promoting color-blind policies. In Inniss's assessment, Canadian color-blindness however ignores the past and present status of black Canadians and thus ultimately inheres to their continuing disadvantage. Michelle Williams also observes that anti-black racism is embedded in the criminal justice system as well.[102] Nor is continuing racism limited to black Canadians or aboriginal communities.[103] It also extends to the racial profiling of Arabs and Muslims.[104]

98 Bruce Porter, *Twenty Years of Equality Rights: Reclaiming Expectations*, 23 WINDSOR Y.B. ACCESS JUST. 145 (2005).

99 Hart Schwartz, *Making Sense of Section 15 of the Charter*, 29 N.J.C.L. 201 (2011).

100 Eisen, *supra* note 96, at 41.

101 Lolita Buckner Inniss, *Toward a Sui Generis View of Black Rights in Canada—Overcoming the Difference-Denial Model of Countering Anti-Black Racism*, 9 BERKELEY J. AFR.-AM. L. & POL'Y 32 (2007).

102 Michelle Y. Williams, *African Nova Scotian Restorative Justice: A Change Has Gotta Come*, 36 DALHOUSIE L.J. 419 (2013).

103 CONSTANCE BACKHOUSE, COLOUR-CODED: A LEGAL HISTORY OF RACISM IN CANADA 1900–1950 (1999).

104 Reem Bahdi, *No Exit: Racial Profiling and Canada's War Against Terrorism*, 41 OSGOODE HALL L.J. 293 (2003).

Dignity as a Touchstone of Equality

Disappointment with the enforcement of Canada's original substantive equality vision has also been noted by Jennifer Koshan and Jonnette Watson Hamilton.[105] Koshan and Hamilton, note that the Supreme Court of Canada has vacillated with new approaches to equality claims every decade, and that the continued reinvention of the Charter has led to a marked lack of success for plaintiffs alleging discrimination. Most troublesome in their view has been the turn towards treating dignity as the touchstone of equality. With viewing the violation of dignity as a measure of discrimination, the perverse effect has been the shift from a focus on social disadvantage to a much too narrow concern with personal feelings. The focus on the feeling of dignity is problematic because it does not account for larger systemic factors at issue. Systemic racism conceives of discrimination as extending beyond the intentional actions of individuals, and instead includes the policies and practices entrenched in established institutions that result in the exclusion or promotion of particular groups. The narrowing of the definition of discrimination and its avoidance of systemic racism hinders the law's ability to fully recognize and address systemic discrimination.

What the demand for a dignity-approach to anti-discrimination law overlooks is how inequality includes indignity but is not reducible to it:[106] "It is just not all there is to it, or even its irreducible core, sine qua non, or floor."[107] For this reason, a dignity approach cannot substitute for the harm of inequality on its own terms. As legal scholar Catharine MacKinnon explains:

> Inequality is always undignified. But reducing its injury to the feeling of indignity in the subordinated person makes it all mental and within the unequally treated person, which tends to cover up, even trivialize, the coercive and injurious external conditions and systemic acts usually involved, the material deprivations and physical harms inflicted by dominant groups, along with the resources and status they benefit from.... [Inequality's] demeaning meanings cannot be ended without also ending its material deprivations. For instance, the harm of unequal pay is not only that it deprives one of dignity, although it can, but that it deprives

105 Jennifer Koshan & Jonnette Watson Hamilton, *The Continual Reinvention of Section 15 of the Charter*, 64 Univ. New Brunswick L.J. 19 (2013).

106 Catharine A. MacKinnon, *Substantive Equality: A Perspective*, 94 Minn. L. Rev. 1, 1–27, 10 (2011).

107 *Id.*

> one of money. Reducing inequality to its dignitary dimension misses too much to be able upon remediation to produce equality.[108]

In short, a dignity approach to discrimination sidelines the concern with material inequality which is the only effective mechanism for addressing racial subordination inasmuch as inequality is always about material hierarchy. Most importantly,

> the inequality exists whether the person subjected to it experiences a loss of dignity or not. Put another way, dignity is a value or feeling. Equality is only secondarily a value or feeling. Primarily it is a fact. Inequality is also a fact.... The injury of inequality is not reducible to feeling bad at its indignity, although we often do. The injury is the harm of the fact of one's equal humanity being denied realization in the world. Fixing the world will fix the way we fell about it.[109]

However, just as the Canadian Charter of Freedoms has been critiqued for not realizing its full transformative potential, other jurisdictions can be similarly critique for their inattention to systemic racism. In this vein, Eddie Bruce-Jones notes that German anti-discrimination law is similarly weak with regard to institutional racism.[110] The lack of efficacy of the German laws is particularly striking given its legal prohibition against "indirect discrimination."[111]

Indirect Discrimination

Indirect discrimination is the use of neutral rules or policies that can have a disparate disadvantageous impact on a protected group. Because indirect discrimination is a claim that does not require proof of an individual intent to discriminate, it is thought to be more conducive to addressing matters of institutional discrimination that facilitate systemic racism. Yet it is not adequate for anti-discrimination laws to simply prohibit indirect discrimination in its text, without having a careful consideration of the forms of evidence that will be deemed appropriate. Direct discrimination inherently invites evidence of racially derogatory statements while access to public goods (like employment,

108 Catharine A. MacKinnon, Butterfly Politics 464 (2017).

109 *Id.* at 472–73.

110 Bruce-Jones, *supra* note 5.

111 Allgemeines Gleichbehandlungsgesetz [AGG] [General Act on Equal Treatment], Aug. 14, 2006, BGBl. I at 1897 (Ger.).

housing, education, etc.) is denied. In contrast, indirect discrimination puts into question what should be suggestive of discriminatory practices in the absence of inflammatory racial statements.

The United States, the jurisdiction with the longest record of addressing indirect discrimination under what it terms "disparate impact," initially answered this question with a reliance on statistical disparities, which not all jurisdictions are comfortable embracing. In fact, even the United States has vacillated in its willingness to rely upon statistical data as evidence of discrimination. Nevertheless, given the developed United States jurisprudence on statistical evidence, it is often the source of comparison for jurisdictions contemplating indirect discrimination enforcement.

U.S. anti-discrimination law examines statistical evidence in two types of discrimination cases—systemic claims of intentional discrimination and disparate impact claims of indirect discrimination. Statistical evidence about racial disparities across a large group is viewed as relevant to the question of discrimination because the systemic effects of discrimination might otherwise be invisible with a judicial focus on one single plaintiff examined in isolation. In systemic claims of intentional discrimination (also known as systemic disparate treatment), statistics provide circumstantial evidence of intent, or impermissible motivation. They provide a basis from which the court can infer intent.[112] For instance, in the seminal employment discrimination case of *Teamsters v. United States*, the Supreme Court states:

> Statistics showing racial or ethnic imbalance are probative in a case such as this one only because such imbalance is often a telltale sign of purposeful discrimination; absent explanation, it is ordinarily to be expected that nondiscriminatory hiring practices will in time result in a work force more or less representative of the racial and ethnic composition of the population in the community from which employees are hired.[113]

As a result, the Supreme Court suggests that a prima facie case can be established by comparing "the [racial] composition of a work force and that of the general population."[114] Absent a nondiscriminatory reason for the racial disparity, the statistical disparity may be enough to prove discrimination. Thus for

---

112 Village of Arlington Heights v. Metropolitan Housing Development Corp, 429 U.S. 252 (1977).

113 Teamsters v. United States, 431 U.S. 324, 391 n.20 (1977).

114 *Id.*

instance, a racial disparity in the relevant qualified workforce population for an advertised position, and low numbers of hired qualified racial minorities, can be determinative of discrimination.

To rebut a systemic discrimination, one must attack the truth and veracity of the statistical evidence. For example, the sample size may be too small to be statistically significant, or general population statistics may not accurately reflect who was in fact available for the job in question. This prevents the plaintiff's prima facie case of discrimination from being established. Absent a successful attack on the truth and veracity of the statistical evidence, the statistical disparity must be explained away by a legitimate, nondiscriminatory reason—e.g., it resulted solely from a racially neutral test fairly applied to all employees. But adverse effects do not always establish intent because there is no legal requirement that a public sphere like employment or elsewhere be "racially" balanced. The examination of statistics is for assessing racial exclusion not the ideal of inclusion. The ultimate burden remains on the plaintiff to prove intentional discrimination.

In contrast, with disparate impact indirect discrimination, statistics are the bottom line—they provide direct evidence of discrimination. In the United States, *Griggs v. Duke Power Co.*[115] remains one of the most important disparate impact cases. It holds that a claim of unlawful discrimination can be established upon the basis of disparate impact alone. In the employment context this is predicated on the assumption that, over a period of time, there should be little difference between selection and availability data; for example, the racial composition of a nondiscriminatory employer's work force should look very similar to that of its relevant labor market. Hence, statistical disparity in the at-issue jobs can by itself raise a rebuttable presumption of employment discrimination. Unlike disparate treatment intentional discrimination statistics which compare workforce statistics against the labor market, disparate impact indirect discrimination compares actual or predicted passage rates of a specifically challenged neutral practice. For instance, comparing percentages of group members that passed a work test against percentages of non-group members who qualify with a 4/5 rule, means that if the passage rate for group members is 80% or less than the passage rate for non-group members then disparity exists.

Another distinction from the systemic intentional discrimination case use of statistics, is that disparate impact indirect discrimination demands that in addition to showing statistical disparity between availability and selection

115 Griggs v. Duke Power Co., 401 U.S. 424 (1971).

data, the plaintiff also has to demonstrate that the disparity complained of is the result of one or more employment practices. In the U.S. jurisprudence, the belief is that "to hold otherwise would result in employers being potentially liable for the myriad of innocent causes that may lead to statistical imbalances in the composition of their work forces."[116] The defendant may present a business necessity defense that the neutral practice or test is job-related. Or demonstrate that the particular employment practice identified by the plaintiff did not cause the disparity. However, if the plaintiff can show that there are alternatives that are feasible and efficient and will satisfy employer's business interests without similar undesirable adverse racial impact (ex. with a different test, scoring procedure, or practice), then the court can find that the neutral practice or test is actually used as "pretext" for discrimination that is unlawful.

Despite the use of disparate impact indirect discrimination claims over the course of the last five decades, some judges have begun to question and limit the applicability of the claim. For instance, in the 2015 housing discrimination case of *Texas Dept of Housing & Comm Affairs v. Inclusive Communities Project, Inc.*, the Supreme Court, by a five-to-four margin, upheld the application of disparate impact under the Fair Housing Act ("FHA") but imposed significant limitations on its application in practice "to protect potential defendants against abusive disparate-impact claims." In particular, the Court held that a racial imbalance, without more, cannot sustain a claim, and directed lower courts to "examine with care" the claims at the pleadings stage. The Court emphasized the plaintiff's burden to establish a "robust" causal connection between the challenged practice and the alleged disparities. Further, a defendant's justification is "not contrary to the disparate-impact requirement, unless ... artificial, arbitrary, and unnecessary." Finally, "remedial orders" must "concentrate on the elimination of the offending practice" through "race-neutral means." Particularly worrisome is that the Court warned that if the limitations described in its decision are not observed, "the specter of disparate-impact litigation" under the FHA would "[undermine] its own purpose as well as the free-market system and thereby cause "serious constitutional questions." Because the Court's limitations appear in tension with the federal Department of Housing and Urban Development's description of the theory contained in its 2013 disparate-impact rule, commentators expect these issues to be played out in future litigation.[117]

---

116 Watson v. Fort Worth Bank, 487 U.S. 977, 992 (1988).

117 Paul Hancock, *Symposium: The Supreme Court Recognizes but Limits Disparate Impact in its Fair Housing Act Decision*, SCOTUSBLOG (Jun. 26, 2015, 8:58 AM), http://www.scotusblog.com/2015/06/paul-hancock-fha/.

With the Supreme Court's growing hostility disparate impact indirect discrimination claims, plaintiffs will be steered to solely filing individual direct discrimination claims. Individual cases of direct discrimination in the United States require proof of an intent to discriminate where the search is for whether a decision maker made a decision "because of race" rather than based on merits. It is immaterial if the reason was accompanied by other reasons, as long as discrimination was the motivating factor. The inquiry into direct discrimination focuses on the defendant's process of decision-making. Yet, given the inability to accurately ascertain the psychological content of a decision maker's mind, the focus is instead on circumstantial evidence that is considered with a set of shifting burdens of proof. *McDonnell Douglas Corp. v. Green*,[118] is the seminal case for outlining the allocation of proof burdens in these cases. The burden of producing evidence is the focus of the case. The burden of persuading the trier of fact is always on the plaintiff. *McDonnell Douglas* allows a plaintiff to establish a prima facie case for establishing intentional discrimination by:

1) asserting that the discrimination was because of race
2) applied for a job, promotion, job retention etc. and was qualified when decision maker was considering applicants
3) despite his or her qualifications plaintiff was rejected
4) after the rejection the decision maker continued to seek applicants from persons of complainant's qualifications

After establishing a prima facie case, the burden then shifts to the decision maker to show it had some legitimate, non-discriminatory reason for the decision that was made. If the decision maker carries that burden, then plaintiff must prove that the decision maker's stated reason is merely a pretext for discrimination. While the *McDonnell Douglas* standard for making a prima facie case of direct discrimination was meant to assist plaintiffs who only had circumstantial evidence to mount a sufficient case to demand that an employer provide a nondiscriminatory explanation for any adverse treatment, over time U.S. judges have come to demand overt proof of an intent to discriminate that most plaintiffs cannot provide.[119] As discussed in part 1, contemporary judges seemingly believe that the U.S. has become a post-racial society in which instances of true racism as existed before the passage of civil rights laws are rare. For this reason, commentators question the ability of U.S. anti-discrimination law to continue redressing existing racial inequalities.[120]

118 McDonnell Douglas Corp. v. Green 411 US 792 (1973).

119 Haney Lopez, *supra* note 55.

120 John Valery White, *The Activist Insecurity and the Demise of Civil Rights Law*, 63 LA. L. REV. 783 (2003).

Statutory Exceptions to Discrimination

A nation-state's conviction that racism is rare in its society can also influence not only a judiciary's definition of discrimination, but also how a legislature creates statutory exceptions to discrimination. For instance, in Hong Kong's racial discrimination legislation enacted in 2008, a number of statutory exceptions are thought to significantly undermine its efficacy.[121] Specifically, the Racial Discrimination Ordinance exempts employers from being liable for discrimination if an employer asserts that a person's racial identity is a genuine occupational qualification.[122] Puja Kapai notes that such a statutory exception usually opens the door to discrimination, inasmuch as employers rely upon biased stereotypes to justify race-based occupational requirements.[123] Thus, even though the Hong Kong statute does not require that an intent to discriminate be asserted to lodge a racial complaint, the genuine occupational qualification and other exceptions effectively make the statute as challenging for plaintiffs as the U.S. demand for proof of an intent to discriminate. In fact, the number of complaints filed has remained low since the law's 2008 enactment.[124] As a result, Peterson and Loper have noted that international human rights organizations have criticized the Hong Kong legislation as inadequate.[125] However, it is not only a list of exceptions to what is considered discrimination that can influence how meaningfully the law is applied, but also whether the law is enacted within a penal code or civil law, as discussed in the next part.

Part 4: Criminal v. Civil Law

The practicalities of how definitions of discrimination are given meaning are also informed by whether the relevant laws are enacted as part of the criminal or civil law. For instance, despite the variation in the type of legal instruments available across Latin America dedicated to the eradication of

121 Carole J. Petersen & Kelley Loper, *Equal Opportunities Law Reform in Hong Kong: The Impact of International Norms and Civil Society Advocacy*, *in* Reforming Law Reform: Perspectives from Hong Kong and Beyond 173, 173 (Tilbury, Michael et al. ed., 2014).

122 Race Discrimination Ordinance, (2009) Cap. 602 (H.K.), *available at* https://www.elegislation.gov.hk/hk/cap602 (last visited Aug. 29, 2018).

123 Puja Kapai, *Status of Ethnic Minorities in Hong-Kong 1997–2014: The Rights of Ethnic Minorities Under The Law: Equality And Non-Discrimination*, Univ. of Hong-Kong: Cent. for Comp. and Pub. Law (2015).

124 *Id.*

125 Petersen & Loper, *supra* note 121.

racial discrimination (multi-cultural constitutional recognition, collective land titles, affirmative action programs, labor and consumer law protections, etc.), the deployment of criminal law legal sanctions has been most pervasive across the region. In order to understand the Latin American focus on criminal law for addressing racial discrimination, it is first important to describe the constitutional law backdrop against which social justice activists have had to contend.

Constitutional Equality Protections

Most countries in the Latin American region have traditionally relied upon broadly worded constitutional equality provisions as the confirmation that racial inequality has been adequately addressed. An example of the generally worded constitutional provisions that all Latin American countries have with some variation can be seen in Nicaragua's equality provision, which states:

> All people are equal before the law and have the right to equal protection. There will be no discrimination on account of birth, nationality, political belief, race, sex, language, opinion, economic status or social position.

Yet the constitutional equality provisions are rarely applied to the context of racial discrimination, because of the view (discussed in part 1) that "real racism" only truly exists in the United States, and is thus an aberration in Latin American cultures.

Criminal Law Provisions

As a result, there has been a tendency to operationalize constitutional equality principles with enabling legislation located in the criminal law to sanction the culturally aberrational behavior of the presumably few racists that reside in the region. Indeed, the vast majority of countries in Latin America have focused upon criminal law as the vehicle for addressing racial discrimination. César Rodríguez Garavito and Carlos Andrés Baquero Díaz note that all Latin American countries except for Paraguay have passed laws to criminally punish acts of racial discrimination.[126] Given the long histories of ignoring the existence of racism and discrimination in Latin America, it is understandable that the strongest state sanction that criminal law provides would be sought as the symbol of the state's new commitment to recognizing societal

---

126 Cesar Augusto Rodriguez Garavito & Carlos Andres Baquero Diaz Reconocimiento con Redistribución: El Derecho Y la Justicia Étnico-Racial en América Latina 68 (2015).

discrimination. Consequently, criminal law sanctions are often the default anti-discrimination approach because of their strong normative message that the State condemns racism.[127]

As a result, the few criminal prosecutions that have been brought since the social justice movement advocacy in the 1990s for recognition of racial discrimination have been noteworthy. Peru criminally convicted an individual for racial discrimination against an Afro-Peruvian for the first time in 2015.[128] Similarly, Ecuador issued its first prison sentence for racial discrimination against an Afro-Ecuadorian only in 2016.[129]

Unfortunately, other motivations for the public focus on criminal law conflict with fully addressing the sources of racial inequality. For instance, further entrenching the focus on criminal law provisions has been the notion that Latin American nation-states have been innocent of racial wrongdoing. Given the absence of state-mandated Jim Crow segregation in the region, the legal stance toward racism has been to view it as an aberration rather than a systemic part of a national culture.[130] As a result, the legal response has been to treat racism as the work of isolated individuals, who are presumably abnormal in their prejudices. In short, racists are criminals rather than representatives of longstanding racist cultural norms. Garavito and Díaz conclude that the use of criminal law individualizes racism and fails to challenge the structural causes of racial inequality.[131]

This also helps to explain why the large majority of hate speech laws in Latin America are part of the criminal codes in the region. Unfortunately, limiting the idea of racism to biased words uttered by those labeled as aberrant racists overlooks the structural and institutional aspects of discrimination that operate in the absence of racist commentary. Carlos de la Torre notes with respect to the plight of Afro-Ecuadorians that "[r]educing racism to the hostile words and actions of ignorant, ethnocentric, and parochial individuals, a view that was dominant in American sociology until recently, does not take into account power relations."[132]

---

127 Robert J. Cottrol, The Long, Lingering Shadow: Slavery, Race, and Law in the American Hemisphere (2013).

128 Sentencia No. 479-2015-2JPL-PJ-CSJJU (Peru).

129 Proceso No. 17124-2014-0585 (Ecuador).

130 Tanya Katerí Hernández, Racial Subordination in Latin America: The Role of the State, Customary Law and the New Civil Rights Response 104 (2013).

131 Garavito and Díaz, *supra* note 126, at 92.

132 Carlos de la Torre, *Afro-Ecuadorian Responses to Racism: Between Citizenship and Corporatism*, *in* Neither Enemies nor Friends: Latinos, Blacks, Afro-Latinos 61 (Anani Dzidzienyo & Suzanne Oboler eds., 2005).

Some countries in Latin America maintain a singular criminal approach to discrimination.[133] For example, in the Dominican Republic, the 1997 *Ley contra la Violencia Intrafamiliar* (Law against Interfamily Violence) makes it a crime to inflict unequal or humiliating treatment based on race or ethnicity. Persons found guilty of the crime of discrimination can be imprisoned for a year and one month and a fine of two to three times the minimum wage.[134] In Nicaragua, the Criminal Code penalizes the obstruction of a constitutional right because of race or ethnicity.[135] The penalty is six months to one year of imprisonment. If the racially motivated obstruction of a constitutional right is found to have been publicly promoted, an additional fine can be imposed. The Criminal Code also authorizes the augmentation of a penalty for other crimes when they are racially motivated.[136]

While criminal sanctions suggest a strong normative commitment to the eradication of discrimination, it may, as a practical matter, have had the ironic effect of making the legal system less capable of dealing with the problems of inequality and discrimination. Criminal cases require stronger evidence and a higher burden of proof than civil cases. For instance, in an analysis of Peruvian grievances regarding the experience of filing a criminal complaint of discrimination, it was found that the evidentiary standard for discrimination cases was high and that it is often difficult for a victim to prove that he/she has experienced discrimination.[137] An illustrative case described in the report is that of an individual who lodged a complaint against the police department alleging discrimination for the inappropriate issuance of a traffic ticket because of his race. The public prosecutor indicated that this complaint did not merit a criminal investigation or action because the evidence presented was not enough: the complainant had submitted an affidavit and that of a family member who witnessed the incident. It is difficult to fathom what more the complainant could have submitted to support his allegations. The demand for more is thus emblematic of the Latin American resistance to considering racial discrimination a viable criminal complaint. In fact, in one comprehensive study of all electronically available racial discrimination criminal cases in Brazil from 1998 through 2010, over forty percent of the cases that reached a judicial decision

133 Hernández, *supra* note 130.

134 Ley No. 24-97 (Dominican Republic).

135 Ley No. 641, Criminal Code (Nicar.).

136 Ley No. 641, 13 Nov. 2007, Código Penal [Criminal Code] art. 36.5, La Gaceta, Diario Oficial [L.G.], 4 July 2018 (Nicar.).

137 Defensoria del Pueblo, la Discriminación en el Perú: Problemática, Normatividad Y Tareas Pendientes 119 (2007).

resulted in criminal acquittals.[138] Importantly, the study noted that acquittals were often based on the failure to prove a criminal intent to discriminate.

Even cases where lower courts initially conclude that racism has been committed, are at a high risk for later being vacated by courts of appeal. For example, in Colombia when a councilmember in the municipality of Marsella, Risaralda, was prosecuted for the crime of racial harassment for using the word "cancer" to describe indigenous peoples during debate in the city council involving an indigenous community's occupancy of a one of the town's sports' facility. The lower court initially convicted the accused to 16 months of imprisonment and a fine. However, the court of appeals vacated the judgment as it concluded that the words of the councilmember did not constitute harassment in the terms of the statute and, therefore, his actions were not covered by the Law.[139]

Specifically, the court of appeals found that article 134B of the Penal Code did not prohibit the actions of the councilmember. That provision states:

> Whomever promotes or incites acts, conduct or behavior that constitute harassment, oriented towards causing physical or moral injury to a person, group of persons, community or people, because of their race, ethnicity, religion, nationality, political or philosophical ideology, sex or sexual orientation or disability and other reasons for discrimination, will incur a prison sentence from twelve (12) to thirty six (36) months and a fine from ten (10) to fifteen (15) times the current legal monthly minimum wages, unless the conduct constitutes a felony punishable with a harsher sentence.

The court of appeals found that although the expressions of the councilman were unfortunate, they were not intentionally trying to instigate other people or the members of the council to harass the indigenous community that was occupying the sports' facility or any other marginalized group and, therefore, his actions were not covered by the statute. Here the judicial demand for the equivalent of an overt statement like "I am a racist and it is my intent to discriminate against you," obstructs the court's ability to comprehend that the

---

138 Marta Rodriguez de Assis Machado et al., *Racismo e Insulto Racial na Sociedade Brasileira: Dinâmicas de reconhecimento e invizibilização a partir do direito*, 35.03 Novos Estud. 11 (2016).

139 Joaquín Robles Zabala, *Una Enfermedad Incurable*, Revista Semana (Dec. 15, 2014), https://www.semana.com/opinion/articulo/una-enfermedad-incurable-opinion-joaquin-robles-zabala/412321-3.

context of invoking the indigenous as a fatal disease in a discussion about their unwelcome presence in urban spaces, is inherently a racialization of the group.

Judges and Enforcement

Judges are also impeded in imposing criminal sanctions because of the reluctance of prosecutors to proceed with racial discrimination cases. Latin American criminal justice systems are overloaded with traditional crimes of violence and property crimes. In a system plagued with such problems and systemic inefficiencies, the crimes of racism and racial discrimination have and are likely to continue to be a low priority.

Moreover, entrusting the enforcement of the criminal law to public authorities risks having the law undermined by the complacent inaction of public officials who may harbor the same racial bias as the agents of discrimination. Indeed, commentators have noted that Latin American police officers are often the perpetrators of racial violence against persons of African descent because they see their role as protecting society from "marginal elements" by any means necessary without regard to the rule of law.[140] This is a particular danger in Latin America, where police officers are consistently found to discourage Afro-descendants from filing racial discrimination complaints.[141]

In fact, the statistical data that does exist, illustrates the inadequacy of criminal law structures for fully addressing issues of racial discrimination. For instance, in the case of Bolivia, the Anti-racism Committee, which is a governmental entity dependent upon the Vice-Ministry of Decolonization, indicates that since the adoption of the Law Against Racism and All Forms of Discrimination (Law 045) in 2010, only 1,394 cases of discrimination have been filed. In 2017 alone, there were 219 administrative and criminal complaints of discrimination on the basis of race, gender and other characteristics—of those, 20 have ended up in criminal sentences.[142] Of the 210 cases of discrimination registered in Bolivia, only ten of them were cases of discrimination based on color (Racism). Only 44 of the total cases that year have been resolved.[143]

140 Paulo Sergio Pinheiro, *The Rule of Law and the Underprivileged in Latin America: Introduction, in* THE (UN)RULE OF LAW AND THE UNDERPRIVILEGED IN LATIN AMERICA (Juan E. Mendez, Guillermo O'Donnell & Paulo Sergio Pinheiro eds., 1999).

141 DANIEL M. BRINKS, THE JUDICIAL RESPONSE TO POLICE KILLINGS IN LATIN AMERICA: INEQUALITY AND THE RULE OF LAW (2008); Michael J. Mitchell & Charles H. Wood, *Ironies of Citizenship: Skin Color, Police Brutality, and the Challenge to Democracy in Brazil*, 77 SOCIAL FORCES 1001–20 (1999).

142 La Razon, *Suspenden A Unos 10 Maestros Por Discriminacion*, LA RAZON: SOCIEDAD (Mar. 22, 2018), http://www.la-razon.com/sociedad/Suspenden-maestros-discriminacion_0_2896510324.html.

143 MINISTERIO DE CULTURAS Y TURISMO, 2017.

Civil Law Frameworks

Seth Racusen notes that a civil framework can provide broader theories of discrimination and less burdensome evidentiary standards.[144] In addition, the civil context carries less risk of selective enforcement whereby vulnerable populations are disproportionately targeted for prosecution. This is because, unlike in criminal prosecutions, the state need not be the primary enforcer of the legislation. The contrast between the civil and criminal contexts is best exemplified by the Brazilian case of *Tiririca*, in which the same fact pattern of hate speech yielded success for the plaintiffs in the civil court but not in the criminal court. Francisco Everado Oliveira Silva, whose stage name was Tiririca, is a Brazilian Congressman and former entertainer who released a song with the Sony Music company entitled "*Veja os Cabelos Dela*" ("Look at Her Hair") in 1996. The song was in essence a long tirade against the inherent distasteful animal smell of black women and the ugliness of their natural hair. The lyrics stated in significant part:

> When she passes she calls my attention, but her hair, there's no way no. Her *catinga* [African] (body odor) almost caused me to faint. Look, I cannot stand her odor. Look, look, look at her hair! It looks like a scouring pad for cleaning pans. I already told her to wash herself. But she insisted and didn't want to listen to me. This smelly *negra* (Black woman) ... Stinking animal that smells worse than a skunk.

The black feminist NGO Criola, in conjunction with the NGO CEAP (*Centro de Articulação de Populações Marginalizadas*), and a number of other social justice organizations filed lawsuits against the singer and Sony Music company in both criminal and civil courts. In the criminal court action, the plaintiff filed a complaint of racism. The plaintiff lost because the judge found that there was no criminal intent to offend black women. The criminal law standard was too high to overcome given the infrequency with which individuals overtly state their intent to discriminate before nonparty witnesses. As a result, the song remained in circulation for commercial sale.

In contrast, the civil court action was successful. The civil public action was filed pursuant to Article 3 of the Constitution, which states that the national

144 Seth Racusen, A Mulato Cannot Be Prejudiced: The Legal Construction of Racial Discrimination in Contemporary Brazil, 87–8 (2002) (unpublished Ph.D. dissertation, Massachusetts Institute of Technology); Seth Racusen *"Making the 'Impossible' Determination: Flexible Identity and Targeted Opportunity in Contemporary Brazil*, 36 CONN. L. REV. 787, 787–829 (2004).

objective is "to promote the well-being of all without prejudice as to origin, race, sex, color, age, and any other form of discrimination." The case sought to protect the diffuse and collective rights of black women to be free of discrimination. Diffuse rights are a category of legal rights that provide guarantees to a group of individuals who have common legal interests despite being dispersed within the political community.[145] Free of the criminal context, which requires a finding of intent to discriminate, the civil court held that the defendant's authorship of the lyrics was discriminatory itself because the words inherently provoke feelings of humiliation in black women.[146] The court took note that because the singer, Tiririca, was also a popular entertainer for children (who was often nationally televised in a clown costume), the insulting and injurious content of the song was also prejudicial to the formation of black youth.

As compensation for the moral damages of collective emotional harm to dignity, in 2008, the court ordered payment of 300,000 reais in addition to attorney's fees and costs. In 2012, the court revised the monetary judgment to include sums retroactive to the date the case was filed in 1997, thereby raising the judgment to 1.2 million reais. In civil law legal systems like Brazil's, moral damages are nonpecuniary damages that compensate for the injury of emotional distress from harm to one's honor or reputation.[147] Often, moral damages are not available for every sort of tort action, but only for those that create dignitary harm. The monetary payment for the damage to the collective equality interest of black women was paid to the Federal Ministry of Justice's Fund for the Defense of Diffuse Rights, for the creation of educational antiracism youth programs disseminated through radio, television, film, and printed materials for elementary schools in the state.

What the *Tiririca* case demonstrates is that in the civil context, the absence of the imprisonment feature enables a judge to consider more nuanced perspectives about racial equality when deciding whether the discrimination that has been historically prevalent in Latin America but invisible as "culture" should be actionable. A civil framework can provide broader theories of discrimination and less burdensome evidentiary standards. In addition, the civil context carries less risk of selective enforcement whereby vulnerable populations are disproportionately targeted for prosecution. This is because, unlike in criminal prosecutions, the state need not be the primary enforcer of the

145 Lei No. 7.347, de 24 Julho 1985 (Brazil).

146 T.J.R.J., Embargos Infringentes No. 2005.005.00060 (Braz.).

147 Saul Litvinoff, Moral Damages, 38 LA. L. REV. 1, 1–28 (1977); Jorge A Vargas, *Moral Damages Under the Civil Law of Mexico: Are These Damages Equivalent to U.S. Punitive Damages?*, 35 UNIV. MIAMI INTER-AMERICAN L. REV. 193 (2004).

legislation. Yet, because of the prevalent notion that criminal laws against discrimination show how serious the state is about racism, the development of civil law measures across the region has been slow and their reach has been modest.

The few criminal law racial discrimination cases that have been successful have had inflammatory factual allegations that even the most reticent of courts would find hard to ignore. For instance, in Ecuador, where Afro-Ecuadorians are often ignored and viewed as not inherently Ecuadorian, only the most extreme of racial discrimination actions will be understood as appropriate for criminal enforcement. It was not until July 5, 2016, that Ecuador imposed its first prison sentence for the crime of racial discrimination. In *Michael Arce Méndez v. Fernando Encalada Parrales*, a prison sentence of five months and twenty-four days was issued for the racial hate which an armed forces lieutenant committed against a former cadet at a military school.[148] Mr. Arce Méndez, who dreamed of becoming Ecuador's first Afro-Ecuadorian General, started military school in October, 2011, after successfully completing admissions examinations. Mr. Arce Méndez and other witnesses described the unfair, cruel treatment he received under his instructor, Lt. Encalada Parrales. Lt. Encalada Parrales told Mr. Arce Méndez that no "black" person would become a military official, and then proceeded to harass him until he would resign from the school. The harassment took the form of not allowing cadet Méndez to sleep, forcing him to jog while other cadets were sleeping, not allowing him to eat with the other cadets, not giving him enough time to eat, forcing him to eat on the floor, in addition to many other physical forms of harassment while he was called a "lazy black" and other derogatory race-related terms. Cadet Méndez eventually resigned from the school and made a claim with the Public Defender's Office.

Given the outrageous conduct of a public figure like Lt. Encalada Parrales, it is understandable why the court did not hesitate to make a finding of racial discrimination worthy of imposing a criminal sentence along with payment of psychological treatment, damages and litigation costs. Not only was the victim's physical well-being under assault, a psychological examination also found that cadet Méndez had suffered psychologically as well with a lingering post-traumatic disorder. Other victims of racial discrimination that have been denied opportunities because of their race but absent the physical violence have not been as successful in deploying the criminal law to vindicate their equality rights.

148 Proceso No. 17124-2014-0585 (Ecuador).

Absent physical violence, the racial discrimination allegations must be close to extraordinarily outrageous to be warranted justiciable. For instance, in Peru's first successful prosecution for racial discrimination, the Afro-Peruvian victim was targeted with outright fraud. In the 2015 case of *Azucena Asunción Algendones v. Luis Alberto Perez Peralta*, Azucena Asunción Algendones, secretary at the Municipal Water and Sewer Services Company of Huancayo, which is known as Sedam Huancato S.A., was engaging in her regular conduct of business when co-worker Judith Perez Huaynate alluded to Algendones as a "negra cocodrilo" (black crocodile) while also making insulting gestures towards her. When Algendones asked that Huaynate apologize to her, Huaynate stated that her comment was more of an insult to a crocodile than to Algendones.[149] Algendones alerted both her general manager, Luis Perez Peralta, and subsequently Humans Resources manager, Augusto Santisteban Garcia, about the occurrence with co-worker Huaynate. Despite these supervisors noting that Huaynate had committed a racist act against Algendones, not only was Huaynate not punished, but the supervisors also dismissed the case, thus failing to resolve the issue. Sedam officials then attempted to punish Algendones for reporting this racist occurrence by framing her for multiple thefts within the company and subsequently firing her in 2013. This was done after Algendones had contacted government authorities about the 2012 incident which had led to an investigation of the facilities.

In turn, Algendones filed charges against officials Peralta and Garcia pursuant to Peruvian racial discrimination statutes. She did this by reporting this incident to the Alert Against Racism website, a government site that investigates instances of racial discrimination, to which she was given legal assistance by the Center for Development of Black Peruvian Women. On November 13, 2015, the controlling federal court in Junin state ruled in Algendones's favor, and in turn sentenced Peralta and Garcia to serve three years in prison as well as pay fines of $1,500. In addition, both officials were barred from holding public office for two years.

Yet, despite the restrictions that the criminal law context places on the pursuit of racial equality, it does provide for some advantages that are worthy of consideration. In Julie Suk's assessment of the French penal code discrimination law, she notes that for ethnic minorities whose social exclusion has long been ignored, having racial discrimination classified as criminal is a powerful expression of the State's condemnation of what was previously disregarded.[150]

---

149 Sentencia No. 479-2015-2JPL-PJ-CSJJU (Peru).

150 Julie Chi-hye Suk, *Equal by Comparison: Unsettling Assumptions of Antidiscrimination Law*, 55 AM. J. COMP. L. 295 (2007).

Moreover, the view of acts of discrimination as criminal, situates the Republic itself as the injured party, and the prosecutor's office as defending the interests of the State to eradicate racism. Such symbolism has the potential to educate the public about how it should alter its treatment of ethnic minorities. Another benefit of housing anti-discrimination law in the criminal system is that the publicly funded enforcement apparatus of the government's prosecutor office, can provide greater access to the legal system given the dearth of attorneys willing to take on the complexities of a discrimination case or wait for the uncertain remuneration of a contingency fee arrangement as exists in the civil law context. Yet whether anti-discrimination law is a penal code provision or civil, both have been similarly critiqued for inadequately attending to plaintiffs whose racial claim is simultaneously affected by other aspects of discrimination, like gender or disability etc. This concern with multiple intersectional discrimination is explored in the next part.

Part 5: Multiple Discrimination/Intersectionality

Traditional legal theory and anti-discrimination law have rigidly viewed individuals in categorically simplistic terms such that a human being either has a gender or a race but rarely both. A number of scholars have detailed the ways in which the legal system's narrow focus on single categorical sources of discrimination have obscured the way multiple sources of discrimination can simultaneously and uniquely affect an individual living at the intersection of multiple categories.[151] Women of color have been particularly disadvantaged by the single category approach to discrimination inasmuch as the differentiation they experience is often both about race and gender, but judges often refuse to examine evidence of both under a claim for racial discrimination or a claim of gender discrimination.[152]

151 *See* Kimberlé Crenshaw, *Mapping the Margins: Intersectionality, Identity Politics, and Violence Against Women of Color*, 43 STAN. L. REV. 1242, 1241–42 (1991). *See also* Angela P. Harris, *Race and Essentialism in Feminist Legal Theory*, 42 STAN. L. REV. 581 (1990), Berta Esperanza Hernandez-Truyol, *Building Bridges – Latinas and Latinos at the Crossroads: Realities, Rhetoric, and Replacement*, 25 COLUM. HUM. RTS. L. REV. 369 (1994).

152 *See* Cathy Scarborough, Note, *Conceptualizing Black Women's Employment Experiences*, 98 YALE L.J. 1457 (1989); Judy Scales-Trent, *Black Women and the Constitution: Finding Our Place, Asserting Our Rights*, 24 HARV. C.R.-C.L. L. REV. 9 (1989). *See also* Kathryn Abrams, *Title VII and the Complex Female Subject*, 92 MICH. L. REV. 2479 (1994); Elizabeth M. Iglesias, *Structures of Subordination: Women of Color at the Intersection of Title VII and the NLRA. Not!*, 28 HARV. C.R.-C.L.L. REV. 395, 395–503 (1993).

Sex-plus Claims

For example, the United States 8th Circuit Court of Appeals provides no claim for a Black woman whose employer systematically fires or fails to promote Black women but who hires and promotes white women and Black men. The 8th Circuit affirmed this logic when it failed to critique the unitary analysis of the lower court decision in *DeGraffenreid v. General Motors*. The lower court adamantly refused to examine the ways in which discrimination against Black women can occur because of their status as women of color that is distinct from the sex discrimination white women experience and the race discrimination men of color experience, because it is a symbiosis of both sex discrimination and race discrimination. The court explicitly stated that "this lawsuit must be examined to see if it states a cause of action for race discrimination, sex discrimination, or alternatively either, but not a combination of both."[153]

A few other courts have instead tried to accommodate the unique combination of discrimination claims of women of color by instead allowing the women to articulate their harms as a "sex-plus" claim.[154] But a number of commentators have observed that the sex-plus framework also misapprehends the intersectional nature of the discrimination against women.[155] This is because sex-plus claims use sex as the main method of analysis and subordinate race to a secondary factor as if it were merely an aggravating element to a "traditional"/white female sex discrimination claim. Sex-plus claims are particularly ineffective for women of color when a jurisdiction follows the *Judge v. Marsh* holding of limiting sex-plus pleading to just one "plus" factor.[156] The *Judge* limitation thereby hampers a judicial understanding of the ways in which discrimination is a holistic dynamic that cannot be compartmentalized neatly for women who can be simultaneously located at many sites of oppression like gender, race, national origin, age, sexuality, disability etc.

Gay men and lesbians of color experience a similar judicial schism.[157] As legal scholar Suzanne Goldberg so accurately states "courts have often disregarded that multidimensionality [of a plaintiff's multiplicity of identity categories] and instead dissected the plaintiff, analyzing each protected trait separately rather than recognizing and responding to the discrimination

153 Degraffenreid v. GM Assembly Div., 413 F. Supp. 142, 143 (E.D. Mo. 1976), aff'd in part, rev'd in part and remanded, 558 F.2d 480 (8th Cir. 1977).

154 Jefferies v. Harris Cty. Cmty. Action Ass'n, 615 F.2d 1025 (5th Cir. 1980).

155 Scarborough, *supra* note 152 at 1457–1478.

156 Judge v. Marsh, 649 F. Supp. 770 (D.D.C. 1986).

157 *See, e.g.*, Williamson v. A.G. Edwards, 876 F.2d 69 (8th Cir. 1989) (rejecting discrimination claim by Black gay man on grounds that the discrimination suffered related to plaintiff's sexual orientation rather than race).

based on all of the targeted traits as a synergistic whole."[158] In short, while civil rights legislation is flexible enough to encompass the complexity of overlapping forms of discrimination, the judiciary has been resistant to formulating a mechanism for adequately examining such complexity in its totality.

Intersectionality Theory

Intersectionality theory underscores the necessity of seeing the interactive reality of individuals as raced and gendered in ways that makes their experiences not simply a sum total of characteristics like race and gender, but instead a unique reality with a unique form of subordination. Intersectionality "means the examination of race, sex, class, national origin, and sexual orientation, and how their combination plays out in various settings."[159] The origins of intersectionality theory are rooted in the African American feminist analysis of how racism differentially forms the gender experiences of Black women.[160] In particular, Black feminists documented the ways in which stereotypes about Black women are distinct from those of white women and Black men.[161] Specifically, Black women from slavery through the present have been depicted as sexually promiscuous women who are natural whores. Historically they symbolized sexual savages, and "the embodiment of female evil and sexual lust,"[162] in contradistinction to the stereotypes of white women as inherently respectable and pure.[163] Legal scholar Kimberlé Crenshaw is at the vanguard of incorporating Black feminist writings into her legal analysis for the construction of intersectionality theory. With the incites of Black feminism in mind, Crenshaw articulates the legal dilemma of women of color who are multiply-burdened and have discrimination claims that cannot be understood as resulting

158 Suzanne B. Goldberg, *On Making Anti-Essentialist Arguments in Court*, 81 OREGON L. REV. 629, 629–661 (2005).

159 RICHARD DELGADO & JEAN STEFANCIC, CRITICAL RACE THEORY: AN INTRODUCTION 51 (2001).

160 BELL HOOKS, AIN'T I A WOMAN: BLACK WOMEN AND FEMINISM (1981); ALL THE WOMEN ARE WHITE, ALL THE BLACKS ARE MEN, BUT SOME OF US ARE BRAVE: BLACK WOMEN'S STUDIES (Gloria T. Hull, Patricia Bell Scott & Barbara Smith, eds., 1982); Lugones, Maria C. & Elizabeth V. Spelman, *Have We Got A Theory For You! Feminist Theory, Cultural Imperialism And The Demand For The 'Woman's Voice'*, 6 WOMEN'S STUD. INT'L F. 573, 573–581 (1983); ELIZABETH V. SPELMAN, INESSENTIAL WOMAN: PROBLEMS OF EXCLUSION IN FEMINIST THOUGHT (1988).

161 K. SUE JEWELL, FROM MAMMY TO MISS AMERICA AND BEYOND: CULTURAL IMAGES AND THE SHAPING OF U.S. SOCIAL POLICY (1993).

162 PATRICIA HILL COLLINS, BLACK FEMINIST THOUGHT: KNOWLEDGE, CONSCIOUSNESS, AND THE POLITICS OF EMPOWERMENT (1990).

163 Beverly Balos & Mary Louise Fellows, *A Matter of Prostitution: Becoming Respectable*, 74 NYU L REV. 1220 (1999).

from discrete sources of discrimination. This dynamic is aptly elucidated by Crenshaw's analogy to a traffic intersection:

> Discrimination, like traffic through an intersection, may flow in one direction, and it may flow in another. If an accident happens in an intersection, it can be caused by cars traveling from any number of directions and, sometimes, from all of them.[164]

Other legal scholars have thereafter continued to develop intersectionality theory to encompass the legal issues of all women of color. For example, Trina Grillo explicitly uses intersectionality theory to discuss the nature of multiracial identity within Black movements[165] and Laura Padilla similarly uses the theory to situate women of color in the affirmative action dialogue.[166]

While legal scholars have begun to actively apply intersectionality approaches to their own research, intersectionality theory has largely been absent as an explicit mode of analysis by U.S. jurists because of its absence from the text of anti-discrimination law. For instance, in order to prevail on a Civil Rights Act of 1964 Title VII statutory claim of discrimination, a plaintiff must demonstrate that he or she has a particular identity trait protected by the legislation (like race or gender) and that he or she has been targeted for discrimination based on that trait.[167] Rachel Kahn Best and her coauthors examined 35 years' worth of federal employment discrimination cases in the United States and found that plaintiffs who make intersectional claims are only half as likely to win their cases as other plaintiffs.[168] Moreover, nonwhite women are less likely to win their cases than any other demographic group. As a result Best and her coauthors conclude that "antidiscrimination lawsuits

---

164 Crenshaw, *supra* note 151, at 149.

165 Trina Grillo, *Anti-essentialism and Intersectionality: Tools to Dismantle The Master's House*, 10 BERKELEY WOMEN'S L.J. 16, 16–30 (1995).

166 Laura Padilla, *Intersectionality and Positionality: Situating Women of Color in the Affirmative Action Dialogue*, 66 FORDHAM L. REV. 843, 843–929.

167 *See* McDonnell Douglas Corp. v. Green, 411 U.S. 792, 802 (1973) (explaining first requirement for plaintiff's prima facie case under Title VII's prohibition against race discrimination as showing "that he belongs to a racial minority"); Int'l Bd. of Teamsters v. United States, 431 U.S. 324, 358 (1977) ("The importance of McDonnell Douglas lies … in its recognition of the general principle that any Title VII plaintiff must carry the initial burden of offering evidence adequate to create an inference that an employment discrimination decision was based on a discriminatory criterion illegal under the Act.").

168 Rachel Kahn Best et al., *Multiple Disadvantages: An Empirical Test of Intersectionality Theory in EEO Litigation*, 45 LAW & SOCIETY REV. 991 (2011).

provide the least protection for those who already suffer multiple social advantages."[169]

In contrast, some jurisdictions explicitly incorporate the concept of intersectionality into the text of their anti-discrimination law. The European Union does so with the terminology of "multiple discrimination."[170] Yet the term is not defined nor is any guidance provided regarding how such claims should be processed.[171] In fact, Iyiola Solanke notes that even with the guidance of the EU for drafting the content of discrimination legislation it has been difficult to translate the goal of intersectionality into a legal remedy in Europe.[172] This is because many jurists still continue to apply a single ground form of analysis to intersectional claims in ways that hinder a full inquiry into the complexity of the claim. For instance, judicial insistence that multiple grounds each be considered separately from one another with disaggregated presentations of evidence, underappreciates the synergistic dynamic of how multiple grounds of discrimination interact with one another.[173] A judicial demand that evidence of gender discrimination be disentangled from evidence of racial discrimination, misses how those forms of discrimination mutually interact and do not have separate evidentiary bases. It is to be hoped that with time, more jurisdictions will come to better understand the complexity of multiple discrimination and consider the evidence appropriately. But whether a claim of discrimination is based upon multiple intersectional categories or race singularly, the question of what is the most effective remedy remains. The next part explores the race specific questions of the affirmative action/positive action remedy.

Part 6: Affirmative/Positive Action Remedies for Race Discrimination

The variation in how jurisdictions navigate the legal treatment of policies of social inclusion known interchangeably as affirmative action, positive action,

169 *Id.* at 992.

170 European Union Non-Discrimination Law and Intersectionality: Investigating the Triangle of Racial, Gender and Disability Discrimination (Dagmar Schiek & Anna Lawson eds., 2011).

171 Erica Howard, The EU Race Directive: Developing the protection against racial discrimination within the EU (2010).

172 Iyiola Solanke, Discrimination as Stigma: A Theory of Anti-discrimination Law (2017).

173 Isabelle Carles et al., *Gendered Experiences of Racial Discrimination: Comparative Socio-Legal Research, in* European Union Non-Discrimination Law and Intersectionality 227, 238 (Dagmar Schiek & Anna Lawson eds., 2011).

and positive discrimination, is initially influenced by the inclusion or absence of an explicit textual endorsement. For instance, in South Africa the Constitution explicitly authorizes "measures designed to protect or advance persons or categories of persons" to promote equality.[174] This is because affirmative action is viewed as a form of reparations for the many years of government imposed apartheid.[175] In addition, the South African Employment Equity Act of 1998, states that it is "not unfair discrimination" to "take affirmative measures consistent with the purposes of this Act [which is] to ensure equitable representation in all occupational levels in the workforce [with] preferential treatment and numerical goals, but exclude quotas."[176] The later enactment of a more comprehensive Equality Act created Equality Courts and recognized an affirmative duty of the State to promote equality and outline affirmative measures for the historically disadvantaged.[177] With such explicit approbation of affirmative action measures within South African laws, its Constitutional Court jurisprudence views affirmative action as an integral part of equality and not as a discriminatory derogation from an individual right.[178]

Affirmative Action

The South African context thus contrasts starkly with the contentious battle over affirmative action that exists in the United States and to a lesser degree in other jurisdictions. Some detail about the U.S. context is warranted here in light of how often other jurisdictions reference it either with disdain or admiration regarding the topic of affirmative action. While India innovated the concept of reservations, comparatists tend to focus on the United States when discussing affirmative action.

The term "affirmative action" was first used officially by President Kennedy in a 1961 executive order that created the Committee on Equal Employment Opportunity and was designed to encourage contractors on projects financed with federal funds to racially integrate their workforces. Kennedy's executive order declared that federal contractors should "take affirmative action to ensure that applicants are employed, and employees are treated during their

174 S. AFR. CONST., 1996 § 9.

175 Linda Human, *Affirmative Action as Reparations for Past Employment Discrimination in South Africa: Imperfect and Complex*, *in* WHEN SORRY ISN'T ENOUGH: THE CONTROVERSY OVER APOLOGIES AND REPARATIONS FOR HUMAN INJUSTICE 506 (Roy L. Brooks ed., 1999).

176 Employment Equity Act 55 of 1998 §§ 6, 15 (S. Afr.).

177 The Promotion of Equality and Prevention of Unfair Discrimination Act of 2000, Equality Act 4 of 2000 (S. Afr.).

178 du Toit, *supra* note 95, at 437.

employment, without regard to race, creed, color or national origin."[179] The original goal of the civil rights movement had been "color-blind" laws. However, many activists came to believe that simply ending a long-standing policy of discrimination did not go far enough. They were persuaded that affirmative, or proactive, measures to increase equality were necessary. As President Johnson stated in a 1965 speech at Howard University, "You do not take a person who, for years, has been hobbled by chains and liberate him, bring him up to the starting line of a race and say, 'you are free to compete with all the others,' and still justly believe that you have been completely fair." President Nixon was the first to implement federal policies designed to guarantee minority hiring. Responding to continuing racial inequalities in the workforce, the Nixon administration in 1969 developed the Philadelphia Plan requiring that contractors on federally assisted projects set specific goals for hiring minorities. Federal courts upheld this plan in 1970 and 1971.

Positive Discrimination

Starting in the mid-1990s, U.S. politicians and grassroots groups began to attack affirmative action at the state level with some success. The regents of the University of California system voted in 1995 to end all affirmative action in hiring and admissions, and minority enrollment in the system's entering undergraduate class plummeted in 1998, when the changes took effect. In 1996, California voters approved Proposition 209, an initiative that ended affirmative action throughout the state in public hiring, purchasing, and other government business. In 1998, Washington State voters passed Initiative 200, a measure that banned affirmative action in state and local government hiring, contracting, and education. Such measures exist in several other states as well. The Supreme Court effectively gave states license to continue issuing such bans with its 2014 decision to uphold the state ban on affirmative action in the state of Michigan, in the case of *Schuette v. BAMN*. The Court held that a public ballot initiated amendment to the Michigan State constitution that bans the use of affirmative action at public universities is not a state action that inflicts injury on racial minorities in violation of the Equal Protection Clause of the United States constitution.[180] In doing so, the Supreme Court gave license to any other state to ban race-based affirmative action as well. Eight states currently ban race-based affirmative action at all public universities. California, Washington, Michigan, Nebraska, Arizona, and Oklahoma all passed bans through voter

179 Exec. Order No. 10,925, 26 Fed. Reg. 1977 (Mar. 6, 1961).

180 Schuette v. Coal. to Defend Affirmative Action, 572 U.S. 291 (2014).

referendums. In Florida, Governor Jeb Bush issued an executive order creating the ban.[181] Colorado proposed a ban that was narrowly defeated in 2008.[182]

Similarly, federal courts have also been considering lawsuits from white students denied admission to state universities with affirmative action programs. In some cases, the courts have invalidated such programs on the grounds that they promote reverse racial discrimination. For example, in *Hopwood v. Texas* (1996) a federal appeals court barred the University of Texas Law School from "any consideration of race or ethnicity" in its admissions decisions. As in California, the termination of the school's affirmative action program led to a sharp drop in minority enrollment.

Yet in 2003 the Supreme Court, in the case of *Grutter v. Bollinger*, reaffirmed the premise that affirmative action was constitutionally permissible because the state has a compelling interest in assuring racial diversity. In *Grutter v. Bollinger*, the affirmative action policy for law school admissions at the University of Michigan had been challenged. In the 5 to 4 majority decision Justice Sandra Day O'Connor wrote, "In order to cultivate a set of leaders with legitimacy in the eyes of the citizenry, it is necessary that the path to leadership be visibly open to talented and qualified individuals of every race and ethnicity." Amicus (friend of the court) briefs from the heads of major corporations and from retired military officers argued that affirmative action was essential to produce qualified corporate managers and military leaders and to encourage industrial innovation. These amicus briefs and Justice O'Connor's references to them in her opinion suggest that affirmative action has become a key tool not only to achieve greater equality in the nation but also to help manage sustained economic growth and secure the national defense.

However, on the same day the Supreme Court's *Grutter* decision validated the use of affirmative action in the University of Michigan's law school admissions policy, the Court also issued a separate decision rejecting the affirmative action program used in the University of Michigan's undergraduate program, which was challenged in *Gratz v. Bollinger*. The undergraduate program used a point system in deciding how to weigh applicants, with minority applicants receiving a number of points for the diversity of their racial backgrounds. The Court ruled that this method was too "mechanistic" and amounted to a quota system. The law school program, the Court said, was permissible because it

181 A.R.S. Const. art. II, § 36; Cal Const., art. I, § 31; MCLS Const. art. I, § 26; OK Const. art. 2, § 36A; Ne. Const. art. I, § 30; Rev. Code Wash. (ARCW) (2017) § 49.60.400; N.H. Rev. Stat. Ann. § 21-I:52 (2017); Fla. Exec. Order No. 99–281 (Nov. 9, 1999).

182 Colorado Discrimination and Preferential Treatment By Governments, Initiative 46 (2008), BALOTPEDIA, https://ballotpedia.org/Colorado_Discrimination_and_Preferential_Treatment_by_Governments,_Initiative_46_(2008) (last modified Sept. 3, 2013).

evaluated each applicant individually and used race as one of many factors in deciding whom to admit.

Simultaneously, civil rights organizations hailed the *Grutter* decision because it clearly reaffirmed the value of affirmative action programs even though it could not overturn state laws that prohibit affirmative action, such as those in California and Washington. Opponents of affirmative action vowed to continue fighting and noted the Court's opinion that "enshrining a permanent justification of racial preferences would offend [the] equal protection principle" of the Constitution. "We expect that 25 years from now, the use of racial preferences will no longer be necessary to further the interest approved today," O'Connor wrote.

Indeed, the Supreme Court further narrowed the ability of universities to use affirmative action programs in the 2013 case of *Fisher v. University of Texas at Austin*.[183] In *Fisher*, the Court affirmed the process of considering race as a factor amongst others in a public university's admission efforts to achieve a more diverse student body. But the Court went on to specify that the specific admission process of a university is still subject to strict judicial scrutiny in its implementation to prove that the program is narrowly tailored to pursuing the goal of diversity. The *Fisher* decision narrowed the ability to effectively pursue integration with race-conscious policies by stating that in the judicial assessment of a program the university is not entitled to deference or a presumption of good faith in its operation of the program.

The restrictions on affirmative action were further narrowed in their application to the K-12 setting in the 2007 case of *Parents Involved in Community Schools v. Seattle School District No. 1* and *Meredith v. Jefferson County Board of Education*. The case struck down as unconstitutional affirmative action programs in Seattle, Washington, and Louisville, Kentucky, that used race in assigning K-12 students to public schools. The 5 to 4 majority decision held that assigning students only on the basis of race violated the Equal Protection Clause of the Fourteenth Amendment. While the Court previously held in *Grutter* that racial diversity can be a compelling interest for admission to a university, here the Court held that "[t]he present cases are not governed by *Grutter*." Justice Stephen Breyer, in his dissent, criticized the majority for jeopardizing the progress made regarding racial equality, indicating that "[t]his is a decision that the Court and the nation will come to regret."

The Supreme Court also placed restrictions on affirmative action in the employment context in the June 2009 *Ricci v. DeStefano* case. There, the Court held that the City of New Haven, Connecticut, unlawfully discriminated against white firefighters (and one Hispanic firefighter who joined the lawsuit)

183 Fisher v. Univ. of Tex., 570 U.S. 297 (2013).

on the basis of race when the City discarded promotional examination results because "too many whites and not enough minorities would be promoted." The City claimed that they discarded the results to avoid liability for issuing a test having a disparate impact on minorities—that is, administering a test without intent to discriminate that nevertheless had an adverse effect on minorities. The plaintiff firefighters argued that they were unlawfully discriminated against in violation of Title VII of the Civil Rights Act of 1964 and the Equal Protection Clause of the Fourteenth Amendment.

In the Supreme Court's view, discarding the test results solely on the basis of race was itself discriminatory treatment. The Court, relying on its Equal Protection jurisprudence, held that an employer needs a "strong basis in evidence" to believe that it will face disparate-impact liability unless it takes race-based remedial action in order to lawfully justify a racial classification. This strong basis in evidence can only be established by showing that "the examinations were not job related and consistent with business necessity, or if there existed an equally valid, less-discriminatory alternative that served the City's needs but that the City refused to adopt." The Court found that the City had only a fear of liability, and this was insufficient to meet the strong-basis-in-evidence standard. Therefore, the City was found liable for unlawful discrimination in violation of Title VII of the Civil Rights Act of 1964. Because the action violated the statutory provision, the Court did not address whether the action violated the Equal Protection Clause of the Fourteenth Amendment.

Affirmative Action in Brazil

What comparative analysis has illuminated about the U.S. is that its journey with affirmative action was not preordained by the absence of constitutional or statutory endorsement of such policies. In Julie Suk's comparison of the U.S. and Brazilian path to race-based affirmative action, Suk observes that the Brazilian constitution is similarly devoid of explicit language about the government authorization of affirmative action.[184] Yet, the absence of a textual endorsement of affirmative action in Brazil did not hinder its development after social justice movements exerted pressure on the government to become more racially inclusionary.

Ollie Johnson and Rosana Heringer's volume of collected works describes how Brazil's affirmative action policies began after the nation's return to democratic rule in 1985. The democratization process slowly yielded political space to social movements that were launching public education campaigns

184 Julie C. Suk, *Quotas and Consequences: A Transnational Re-evaluation*, *in* PHILOSOPHICAL FOUNDATIONS OF DISCRIMINATION LAW (Deborah Hellman & Sophia Moreau, eds., 2013).

to raise awareness of racial discrimination and the socioeconomic exclusion of Afro-Brazilians.[185]

The first public policy change took place in 1999 in Porto Alegre, Brazil's sixth-largest city. In that year, the municipal government passed a regulation that 5 percent of the work force of all publicly funded contracts with the city be *negro* (black). Similarly, the state of Bahia, where non-whites constitute 75 percent of the population, adopted a rule requiring one-third of all models and actors in state publicity to be black.

Meanwhile, Brazil's Black Movement was gaining greater international and domestic attention through its participation in venues such as the 2001 United Nations World Conference Against Racism and related gatherings. Changes in federal policy soon followed. Brazil began instituting affirmative action policies on the federal level in 2001, when the Minister of Agrarian Development, Raul Jungmann, issued an executive order mandating that 20 percent of all administrative positions in the ministry be reserved for blacks, as well as 20 percent of the staff of firms contracting with the agency, and that another 20 percent of the firms' staff be women.[186] Just as in the U.S. and elsewhere, there is an understanding that the government should act as a model employer, leading the way for fuller racial integration of the labor market.

Thereafter, the Federal Supreme Court and all other cabinet agencies established affirmative action policies.[187] The Court's affirmative action program set a quota of 20 percent for blacks for public-sector contractors.[188] The Ministry of Justice's affirmative action program reserved 20 percent of supervisory and upper-level advisory positions for black and *pardo* (mixed-race brown) Brazilians. In 2002, a presidential executive decree established the National Affirmative Action Program to encourage the implementation of percentage-based goals for Afro-descendants' participation in federal agencies and the firms under contract with them.

Like the Brazilian federal government, local governments have also launched affirmative action programs. For example, in June 2011, the state of Rio de Janeiro issued a decree establishing a 20 percent set-aside of vacancies

185 Race, Politics, and Education in Brazil: Affirmative Action in Higher Education (Ollie A. Johnson, III & Rosana Heringer eds., 2015).

186 Racusen, *supra* 144, at 811–2.

187 *Id.* at 812–13.

188 Raquel Coelho Lenz Cesar, Acesso A Justiça Para Minorias Racias no Brasil: É a Açao Afirmativa o Melhor Caminho? Riscos e Açertos no Caso da UERJ, 28 (2003) (unpublished Ph.D. dissertation, State University of Rio de Janeiro).

for blacks and persons of Indigenous descent in the public examinations for civil service positions in the state government.[189]

What is particularly noteworthy about Brazil is that it has the most extensive set of university affirmative action programs in Latin America that target Afro-descendants. By August 2010, at least 80 public universities in Brazil had adopted affirmative action policies. The structures of the current programs vary.[190] Some only target Afro-Brazilian students from public secondary schools as a way of reaching the neediest Afro-Brazilian students; other programs set aside seats for public secondary school graduates of any race and then establish proportional slots by race according to demographic percentages in that state.

Another variation establishes separate quotas for Afro-Brazilian students (from public or private secondary schools), in addition to a quota for public school students of any race. A few universities award extra points to the entrance examination scores of Afro-Brazilian applicants and public secondary school graduates. Both mechanisms ensure that middle-class Afro-Brazilians, who have also been underrepresented in public universities and affected by racial discrimination, will not be excluded by class or socioeconomic considerations.

So far, Brazilian courts have upheld the laws against a number of challenges. On April 26, 2012, in a case that challenged the University of Brasilia's affirmative action policy, the Federal Supreme Court ruled the policy constitutionally valid.[191] The landmark unanimous decision declared such policies essential for the state to fulfill its obligation of ensuring the equality of opportunity for every citizen. One of the 10 participating justices, Minister Luiz Fux, even stated that the constitutional provision establishing the government responsibility "to build a free, just and supportive society" requires the reparation for past damages suffered by Afro-Brazilians, and argued that affirmative action fulfills that constitutional obligation. One week later, the Court also affirmed the constitutionality of the University for All Program (*ProUni*), which provides

189 Decreto No. 43007, de 6 de Junho de 2011 (Brazil). http://p-web01.mp.rj.gov.br/Arquivos/Pagina_Candidato/Decreto_43.007_de_06_de_Junho_de_2011.pdf (accessed July 21, 2013).

190 Seth Racusen, *Fictions of Identity and Brazilian Affirmative Action*, 21 NAT'L BLACK L.J. 1 2009); *Cotas No Brasil: Um Panorama do Aplicação de Políticas Afirmativas Nas Universidades Públicas*, REVISTA ADUSP 43, 6–39 (July, 2008), http://www.scielo.br/pdf/pee/v21n2/2175-3539-pee-21-02-00183.pdf.

191 *STF declared the constitutionality of the quota system at the University of Brasilia*, STF INTERNACIONAL (Federal Supreme Court of Brazil news portal) (Apr. 26, 2012), http://www2.stf.jus.br/portalStfInternacional/cms/destaquesClipping.php?sigla=portalStfDestaque_en_us&idConteudo=207138.

scholarships for Afro-descendant students from low-income families to attend private universities.[192]

After the rulings, in August 2012, the Brazilian state institutionalized affirmative action in all public federal universities with the Law of Social Quotas. The law requires federal public universities to reserve half of all new admission spots for public high school graduates. Half of those reserved spots are set aside for students whose household family income falls below 1.5 times the minimum wage per family member. The law also mandates that within that 50 percent set-aside, spots be reserved for Afro-descendants and persons of Indigenous ancestry, proportional to their relative populations within each state.

Empirical data indicate that the Brazilian affirmative action programs have been successful. For instance, a study of student outcomes at the State University of Campinas found that students from socioeconomically and educationally disadvantaged backgrounds performed relatively better than those from a higher socioeconomic and educational level.[193] The study concluded that the need for hard work when striving for greater opportunity (as in preparing for the university admission examination when coming from an under-resourced public secondary school) creates an "educational resilience" that improves performance once a student is admitted to university. The educational resilience of the less-privileged students resulted in higher grade point averages after only one year of university study in 31 of the 55 possible undergraduate courses.

Overall, the relative performance of the affirmative action students was higher in 48 of the 55 courses. Studies of student outcomes at the University of Brasilia, the State University of North Fluminense, the Federal University of Bahia, the State University of Rio de Janeiro, and the Federal University of Espirito Santo found similar results: affirmative action students succeed once provided the opportunity of admission.

Furthermore, despite conservative media news articles suggesting the contrary, growing numbers of Brazilians and program beneficiaries have come to view affirmative action as positive. Indeed, in the 2010 survey of applicants to the State University of Rio de Janeiro, 85.4 percent of the black and Indigenous affirmative action candidates stated they were in agreement with the

---

192 *Supremo declara constitucionalidade do ProUni*, SECRETARIA DE POLÍTICAS DE PROMOÇÃO DA IGUALDADE RACIAL, ÚLTIMAS NOTÍCIAS (May 4, 2012), http://www.seppir.gov.br/noticias/ultimas_noticias/2012/05/supremo-declara-constitucionalidade-do-prouni.

193 Renato H.L. Pedrosa et al., Academic Performance, Students' Background and Affirmative Action at a Brazilian University, 19 HIGHER EDUC. MGMT. & POL'Y 1, 1–20 (2007).

quota system.[194] In contrast, in 2005, only 66.8 percent of affirmative action candidates stated that the affirmative action policy was a positive matter.[195] In fact, the most common stereotype about the program beneficiaries among students is that they are *cones* (nerds) who prefer to work all the time rather than party.[196] The general student body's respect for the program participants is illustrated by the following law student's reflection: "I can tell you that I'm in the third year and I don't see any real difference between the grades of the quota and non-quota students. Many *cotistas* [quota students] do very well, and they definitely deserve to be here; this fact has made me change my [negative] opinion of quotas in the last few years."[197] Similarly, in a 2007 study of 557 university instructors, the vast majority appreciated that affirmative action had contributed to democratizing the academic space by having it more accurately reflect Brazilian society.[198] Furthermore, many university instructors report that the affirmative action programs do not create racial tension or hostility in the university.[199]

In short, the growth of affirmative action in Brazil can be traced to judicial legal justifications that have emphasized broad-based democratic concern with social inclusion and established the basis for these policies in human rights law. As a result, today affirmative action in Brazil not only has a stronger legal foundation and broader support than in the U.S.; the policies have also led to clearer guideposts for implementation with specifically articulated numerical quotas.[200]

Part 7: Conclusion

Regardless of all the variations in crafting anti-discrimination law that this book has examined across numerous jurisdictions, one commonality that they all share is the manner in which lack of administrative resources to enforce the

194 *Dados Socioculturais 2010*, VESTIBULAR (2010), www.vestibular.uerj.br (tabulation of UERJ sociocultural survey question data).

195 Monica Trevino Gonzalez, *Opportunities and Challenges for the Afro-Brazilian Movement*, in BRAZIL'S NEW RACIAL POLITICS 123, 123–138 (Bernd Reiter & Gladys L. Mitchell eds., 2010).

196 Andre Cicalo, *Nerds and Barbarians: Race and Class Encounters through Affirmative Action in a Brazilian University*, 44 J. LATIN AM. STUD. Issue 2, 235, 235–260 (2012).

197 *Id.* at 256–257.

198 Pedrosa, *supra* note 193.

199 *Id.*

200 Tanya Katerí Hernández, *Affirmative Action in the Americas*, AMERICAS QUARTERLY (Summer 2013), http://www.americasquarterly.org/affirmative-action-in-the-americas.

laws condemns them all to desuetude. This is in part why despite the advances in the use of affirmative action in Brazil, civil rights stakeholders are concerned with whether changes in government personnel will reduce the commitment and thus resources needed for the implementation of affirmative action and other anti-discrimination law measures. Comparisons across jurisdictions bear out the premise that administrative resources influence the efficacy of anti-discrimination laws.

For instance, earlier in part 1, it was noted that despite the fact that Israeli law prohibits discrimination based on a person's military profile or duration of reserve service, many jobs require prior military or army reserve service and thereby exclude most of the Arab minority completely from consideration. Yet when the Israeli Equal Employment Opportunities Commission (EEOC) in Israel was provided with additional resources and expert personnel from Twinning, a European Union initiative, it was successful in overturning one large-scale employer's use of the prohibited military service requirement. Specifically, in *Kadi v. Israel Railways*, the EEOC helped an Israeli Arab sue when the Israeli Railways excluded all job applicants who had not served in the Israeli army.[201] A similar story about the effects of administrative resources for enforcement can be found in most jurisdictions. This is why analysts of European and Irish contexts note that despite having anti-discrimination laws, racial inequality continues to be an issue.[202] In short, comparative anti-discrimination analysis teaches us that to make race equality measures count, nation-states must dedicate resources for enforcement lest the laws lie as dead letter on the page.

References

1997 *Ley contra la Violencia Intrafamiliar* (Law against Interfamily Violence) (Dom. Rep.). 336.

Abrams, Kathryn. *Title VII and the Complex Female Subject*, 92 MICH. L. REV. 2479 (1994).

ALL THE WOMEN ARE WHITE, ALL THE BLACKS ARE MEN, BUT SOME OF US ARE BRAVE: BLACK WOMEN'S STUDIES (Gloria T. Hull, Patricia Bell Scott & Barbara Smith, eds., 1982).

---

201 Yair Qedar, *Sharing experience to bring equal opportunities*, ENPI INFO CENTRE, Feature no. 31 (2010), www.enpi-info.eu.

202 MAKING EQUALITY COUNT (Laurence Bond, Frances McGinnity & Helen Russell, eds., 2010).

Allgemeines Gleichbehandlungsgesetz [AGG] [General Act on Equal Treatment], Aug. 14, 2006, BGBl. I at 1897 (Ger.).

Ana Rita Alves, *(PRÉ) TEXTOS E CONTEXTOS: Media, Periferia e Racialização*, REVISTA DE CIENCIAS SOCIAIS—POLITICA & TRABALHO, n. 44, 91–107 (Jan/June 2016), http://www.periodicos.ufpb.br/index.php/politicaetrabalho/article/view/28632/16531.

Alves, Ana Rita. *Realojar, despejar, guetizar. Arqueologias de uma violência obliterada: habitação e racismo nos relatórios nacionais/internacionais*, CENTRO DE ESTUDOS SOCIAIS DA UNIVERSIDADE DE COIMBRA (Mar. 2018), http://saladeimprensa.ces.uc.pt/?col=opiniao&id=16391#.W3bsUuhKjIV.

ANDERSON, TERRY H. THE PURSUIT OF FAIRNESS: A HISTORY OF AFFIRMATIVE ACTION (2004).

Araújo, Marta, *A Very 'Prudent Integration': White Flight, School Segregation and the Depoliticization of (Anti)Racism*, 19 RACE ETHNICITY & EDUC. 300 (n. 2), 300–323 (2016).

Araújo, Marta, *O silencio do racismo em Portugal: o caso do abuso verbal racista na escola*, *in* UM OLHAR ALÉM DAS FRONTEIRAS: EDUCAÇÃO E RELAÇÕES RACIAIS 77, 77–94 (Nilma Lino Gomes ed. 2007).

Araújo, Marta & Silvia Rodriguez Maeso, *The 'prudent' integration of Roma/Gypsy pupils: segregation and white flight in Portuguese compulsory schooling*, 19 J. RACE ENTHNICITY & EDUC. Issue 2, 300 (2014).

ARUDUO, DEBITO. EMBEDDED RACISM: JAPAN'S VISIBLE MINORITIES AND RACIAL DISCRIMINATION (2015).

Azucena Asuncion Algendones v. Luis Alberto Perez Peralta, Sentencia No. 479-2015-2JPL-PJ-CSJJU (Peru).

BACKHOUSE, CONSTANCE. COLOUR-CODED: A LEGAL HISTORY OF RACISM IN CANADA 1900–1950 (1999).

Bahdi, Reem. *No Exit: Racial Profiling and Canada's War Against Terrorism*, 41 OSGOODE HALL L.J. 293 (2003).

Balos, Beverly & Mary Louise Fellows, *A Matter of Prostitution: Becoming Respectable*, 74 NYU L REV. 1220 (1999).

BANTON, MICHAEL. THE INTERNATIONAL POLITICS OF RACE (2002).

BERREY, ELLEN, ROBERT L. NELSON AND LAURA BETH NIELSEN, RIGHTS ON TRIAL: HOW WORKPLACE DISCRIMINATION LAW PERPETUATES INEQUALITY (2017).

Best, Rachel Kahn et al., *Multiple Disadvantages: An Empirical Test of Intersectionality Theory in EEO Litigation*, 45 L. & SOC'Y REV. 991 (2011).

Board of Education of City School District of New York v. Harris, 444 U.S. 130 (1979).

Bourdieu, Pierre & Loic Wacquant, *Sobre as Artimanhas de Razao Imperialista*, *in* 1 ESTUDOS AFRO-ASIATICOS 15, 15–33 (2002).

BRINKS, DANIEL M. THE JUDICIAL RESPONSE TO POLICE KILLINGS IN LATIN AMERICA: INEQUALITY AND THE RULE OF LAW (2007).

BRUCE-JONES, EDDIE. RACE IN THE SHADOW OF LAW: STATE VIOLENCE IN CONTEMPORARY EUROPE (2017).

BUSSTRA, M.J. THE IMPLICATIONS OF THE RACIAL EQUALITY DIRECTIVE FOR MINORITY PROTECTION WITHIN THE EUROPEAN UNION (2011).

BUT SOME OF US ARE BRAVE: BLACK WOMEN'S STUDIES (Gloria T. Hull et al. eds., 2nd ed. 2016).

Caldwell, Kia Lilly. *'Look at Her Hair': The Body Politics of Black Womanhood in Brazil, in* TRANSFORMING ANTHROPOLOGY 11:18–29 (2008) (translating Portuguese lyrics).

Canadian Charter of Rights and Freedoms, Part I of the Constitution Act, 1982, *being* Schedule B to the Canada Act, 1982, c 11 (UK).

Carles, Isabelle et al., *Gendered Experiences of Racial Discrimination: Comparative Socio-Legal Research, in* EUROPEAN UNION NON-DISCRIMINATION LAW AND INTERSECTIONALITY: INVESTIGATING THE TRIANGLE OF RACIAL, GENDER AND DISABILITY DISCRIMINATION 227 (Dagmar Schiek & Anna Lawson eds., 2011).

CARLSON, LAURA. BRP: COMPARATIVE DISCRIMINATION LAW: HISTORICAL AND THEORETICAL FRAMEWORKS 99–100 (2017).

Castaneda v. Partida, 430 U.S. 482 (1977).

Cho, Sumi. *Post-Racialism*, 94 IOWA L. REV. 1589 (2009).

Cicalo, André, *Nerds and Barbarians: Race and Class Encounters through Affirmative Action in a Brazilian University*, 44 J. LATIN AM. STUD. Issue 2, 235, 235–260. (2012).

COLLINS, PATRICIA HILL. BLACK FEMINIST THOUGHT: KNOWLEDGE, CONSCIOUSNESS, AND THE POLITICS OF EMPOWERMENT (1990).

Constitução Federal [C.F.] [Constitution] art. 3, para. IV (Braz.).

Constitución Política de Colombia, art. 7.

Constitución Política de la República de Nicaragua, art. 27.

Constituição da República Portuguesa, VII Revisão Constitucional (2005) Artigos 13, 46, 59 & 69, http://www.parlamento.pt/Legislacao/PAGINAS/CONSTITUICAOREPUBLICAPORTUGUESA.ASPX.

Cotas No Brasil: Um Panorama do Aplicação de Políticas Afirmativas Nas Universidades Públicas, REVISTA ADUSP 43, 6–39 (July, 2008), http://www.scielo.br/pdf/pee/v21n2/2175-3539-pee-21-02-00183.pdf.

COTTROL, ROBERT J. THE LONG, LINGERING SHADOW: SLAVERY, RACE, AND LAW IN THE AMERICAN HEMISPHERE (2013).

Council Directive 2000/43/EC, 2000 O.J. (L 180), art. 8(1).

Crenshaw, Kimberlé Williams. *Race, Reform, and Retrenchment: Transformation and Legitimation in Antidiscrimination Law*, 101 HARV. L. REV. 1331 (1988).

Crenshaw, Kimberlé. *Demarginalizing the Intersection of Race and Sex: A Black Feminist Critique of Antidiscrimination Doctrine, Feminist Theory and Anti-Racist Politics*, 1989 U. CHI. LEGAL F. 139 (1989).

Crenshaw, Kimberlé. *Mapping the Margins: Intersectionality, Identity Politics, and Violence Against Women of Color*, 43 STAN. L. REV. 1241 (1991).

Crenshaw, Kimberlé. *Race, Gender, and Sexual Harassment*, 65 S. CAL. L. REV. 1467 (1992).

Criminal Code, Art. 134B (Colom.).

Criminal Code, Art. 36.5 (Nicar.).

CURRAN, VIVIAN GROSSWALD. COMPARATIVE LAW: AN INTRODUCTION (Vivian Curran eds., 2002).

Curran, Vivian Grosswald. *Cultural Immersion, Difference and Categories in U.S. Comparative Law*, 46 AM. J. COMP. L. 43 (1998).

Dados Socioculturais 2010, VESTIBULAR (2010), www.vestibular.uerj.br (tabulation of UERJ sociocultural survey question data).

Darity, William, Jr. & Ashwini Deshpande, *Tracing the Divide: Intergroup Disparity Across Countries*, 26(1) E. ECON. J. 75 (2000).

Darity, William, Jr. & Jessica Gordon Nembhard, *Racial and Ethnic Economic Inequality: The International Record*, 90 AM. ECON. REV. 308 (2000).

de la Torre, Carlos. 2005. *Afro-Ecuadorian Responses to Racism: Between Citizenship and Corporatism, in* NEITHER ENEMIES NOR FRIENDS: LATINOS, BLACKS, AFRO-LATINOS (Anani Dzidzienyo & Suzanne Oboler eds., 2005).

Decreto No. 43007, de 6 de Junho de 2011 (Brazil). http://p-web01.mp.rj.gov.br/Arquivos/Pagina_Candidato/Decreto_43.007_de_06_de_Junho_de_2011.pdf (accessed July 21, 2013).

DEFENSORIA DEL PUEBLO, LA DISCRIMINACIÓN EN EL PERÚ: PROBLEMÁTICA, NORMATIVIDAD Y TAREAS PENDIENTES 119 (2007). Peru: Defensoria del Pueblo, Republica Del Peru. 119.

DeGraffenreid v. General Motors Assembly Division, 413 F. Supp. 142 (E.D. Mo. 1976).

DELGADO, RICHARD & JEAN STEFANCIC, CRITICAL RACE THEORY: AN INTRODUCTION (2001).

DIVISÕES PERIGOSAS: POLÍTICAS RACIAS NO BRASIL CONTEMPORÂNEO (Peter Fry et al. eds., 2007).

Du Toit, Darcy. *"Affirmative Action" or "Positive Action" in the Employment Context: Comparing the Interpretation of "Equality" by the European Court of Justice with that of the South African Constitutional Court*, 36 COMP. LAB. L. & POLY J. 423 (2015).

DULITZKY, ARIEL E. *A Region in Denial: Racial Discrimination and Racism in Latin America, in* NEITHER ENEMIES NOR FRIENDS: LATINOS, BLACKS, AFRO-LATINOS 35 (Anani Dzidzienyo & Suzanne Oboler eds., 2005).

Dzidzienyo, Anani. *The Changing World of Brazilian Race Relations?, in* NEITHER ENEMIES NOR FRIENDS 137, 137–55 (Anani Dzidzienyo & Suzanne Oboler eds., 2005).

EDLEY, CHRISTOPHER, JR. NOT ALL BLACK AND WHITE: AFFIRMATIVE ACTION, RACE, AND AMERICAN VALUES (1996).

EEOC v. Chicago Miniature Lamp Works, 947 F.2d 292 (7th Cir. 1991).

Eisen, Jessica. *Grounding Equality in Social Relations: Suspect Classification, Analogous Grounds and Relational Theory*, 42 QUEEN'S L.J. 41 (2017).

Employment (Equal Opportunities) Law 5748-1988 (Isr.).

Employment Equity Act 55 of 1998 §§ 6, 15 (S. Afr.).

Establishing the President's Committee on Equal Employment Opportunity. http://www.thecre.com/fedlaw/legal6/eo10925.htm.

EUROPEAN UNION NON-DISCRIMINATION LAW AND INTERSECTIONALITY: INVESTIGATING THE TRIANGLE OF RACIAL, GENDER AND DISABILITY DISCRIMINATION (Dagmar Schiek & Anna Lawson eds., 2011).

Executive Decree 09–2007 (Honduras).

Exec. Order No. 10,925, 26 Fed. Reg. 1977 (Mar. 8, 1961).

FARKAS, LILLA & ORLAGH O'FARRELL, EU COMMISSION, REVERSING THE BURDEN OF PROOF: PRACTICAL DILEMMAS AT THE EUROPEAN AND NATIONAL LEVEL 60, 60–70 (2014).

Fisher v. University of Texas, 570 U.S. 297 (2013).

Flores, René D. *The Resurgence of Race in Spain: Perceptions of Discrimination Among Immigrants*, 94 SOCIAL FORCES 237 (2015).

FRANKENBERG, GÜNTHER. COMPARATIVE LAW AS CRITIQUE (2016).

Gallo Rojas, Catalina, *Igualdad Sin Cuotas*, EL TIEMPO, 7 (July 12, 2009).

GARAVITO, CÉSAR AUGUSTO RODRIGUEZ & CARLOS ANDRES BAQUERO DIAZ RECONOCIMIENTO CON REDISTRIBUCIÓN: EL DERECHO Y LA JUSTICIA ÉTNICO-RACIAL EN AMÉRICA LATINA 68 (2015).

GLOBAL CRITICAL RACE FEMINISM: AN INTERNATIONAL READER (Adrien Katherine Wing ed., 2000).

Goldberg, Suzanne B. *On Making Anti-Essentialist Arguments in Court*, 81 OREGON L. REV. 629 (2005).

Gonzalez, Monica Trevino. *Opportunities and Challenges for the Afro-Brazilian Movement, in* BRAZIL'S NEW RACIAL POLITICS 123, 123–138 (Bernd Reiter & Gladys L. Mitchell eds., 2010).

Gratz v. Bollinger, 539 U.S. 244 (2003).

Griggs v. Duke Power Co., 401 U.S. 424 (1971).

Grillo, Trina. *Anti-essentialism and Intersectionality: Tools to Dismantle The Master's House*, 10 BERKELEY WOMEN'S L.J. 16, 16–30 (1995).

Grutter v. Bollinger, 539 U.S. 306 (2003).

Guimarães, Antonio Sergio. PRECONCEITO E DISCRIMINACAO: QUEIXAS DE OFENSAS E TRATAMENTO DESIGUAL NOS NEGROS NO BRASIL 35 (1998).

Hancock, Paul. *Symposium: The Supreme Court Recognizes but Limits Disparate Impact in its Fair Housing Act Decision*, SCOTUSBLOG (Jun. 26, 2015, 8:58 AM), http://www.scotusblog.com/2015/06/paul-hancock-fha/.

Haney-López, Ian. *Intentional Blindness*, 87 N.Y.U. L. REV. 1779 (2012).

Harris, Angela P. *Race and Essentialism in Feminist Legal Theory*, 42 STAN. L. REV. 581 (1990).

Haskovec, Jarrett. *A Beast of Burden? The New EU Burden-of-Proof Arrangement in Cases of Employment Discrimination Compared to Existing U.S. Law*, 14 TRANSNAT'L L. & CONTEMP. PROBS. 1069 (2005).

Hazelwood School District v. United States, 433 U.S. 299 (1977).

Hernández, Tanya Katerí, *Affirmative Action in the Americas*, AMERICAS QUARTERLY (Summer 2013), http://www.americasquarterly.org/affirmative-action-in-the-americas.

HERNÁNDEZ, TANYA KATERÍ. RACIAL SUBORDINATION IN LATIN AMERICA: THE ROLE OF THE STATE, CUSTOMARY LAW AND THE NEW CIVIL RIGHTS RESPONSE (2013).

Hernández, Tanya Katerí. *Sexual Harassment and Racial Disparity: The Mutual Construction of Gender and Race*, 4 IOWA J. GENDER, RACE & JUSTICE 183 (2001).

Hernandez-Truyol, Berta Esperanza. *Building Bridges—Latinas and Latinos at the Crossroads: Realities, Rhetoric, and Replacement*, 25 COLUM. HUM. RTS. L. REV. 369 (1994).

HESKET, KATIE ET AL., THE INEQUALITY REPORT: THE PALESTINIAN ARAB MINORITY IN ISRAEL (2011).

Hicks v. Gates Rubber Co., 833 F.2d 1406 (10th Cir. 1987).

Hooker, Juliet, *Afro-Descendant Struggles for Collective Rights in Latin America, in* NEW SOCIAL MOVEMENTS IN THE AFRICAN DIASPORA: CHALLENGING GLOBAL APARTHEID, 279, 279–91 (Leith Mullings ed., 2009).

HOOKS, BELL. AIN'T I A WOMAN: BLACK WOMEN AND FEMINISM (1981).

Hopwood v. Texas, 78 F.3d 932 (5th Cir. 1996).

HOWARD, ERICA. THE EU RACE DIRECTIVE: DEVELOPING THE PROTECTION AGAINST RACIAL DISCRIMINATION WITHIN THE EU (2010).

Human, Linda. *Affirmative Action as Reparations for Past Employment Discrimination in South Africa: Imperfect and Complex, in* WHEN SORRY ISN'T ENOUGH: THE CONTROVERSY OVER APOLOGIES AND REPARATIONS FOR HUMAN INJUSTICE 506 (Roy L. Brooks ed., 1999).

Iberoamérica, ¿una región racista?, BBC MUNDO, October 13, 2005, http://news.bbc.co.uk/hi/spanish/latin_america/newsid_4331000/4331708.stm (hereinafter "Iberoamérica, ¿una región racista?").

Iglesias, Elizabeth M. *Structures of Subordination: Women of Color at the Intersection of Title VII and the NLRA. Not!*, 28 HARV. C.R.-C.L.L. REV. 395, 395–503 (1993).

Inniss, Lolita Buckner. *Toward a Sui Generis View of Black Rights in Canada—Overcoming the Difference-Denial Model of Countering Anti-Black Racism*, 9 BERKELEY J. AFR.-AM. L. & POL'Y 32 (2007).

International Brotherhood of Teamsters v. United States, 431 U.S. 324 (1977).

Jácome, Jorge González. *Esclavitud Perpetua: Constuyendo Una Perspectiva De Raza en el Derecho Constitucional Colombiano*. 55 VNIVERSITAS n.111, 313–35 (2006).

Jagwanth, Sara. *Affirmative Action in A Transformative Context: The South African Experience*, 36 CONN. L. REV. 725 (2004).

Jefferies v. Harris City Community Action Association, 615 F.2d 1025 (5th Cir. 1980).

JEWELL, K. SUE. FROM MAMMY TO MISS AMERICA AND BEYOND: CULTURAL IMAGES AND THE SHAPING OF U.S. SOCIAL POLICY (1993).

Johnson, Lyndon B. *To Fulfill These Rights*, (Commencement Address at Howard University, Washington, D.C., June 4, 1965, *in* PUBLIC PAPERS OF THE PRESIDENTS OF THE UNITED STATES: LYNDON B. JOHNSON 635, 635–640 (Vol. 2, 1965).

Judge v. Marsh, 649 F. Supp. 770 (D.D.C. 1986).

JUDICIAL STUDIES CENTER OF THE AMERICAS, THE JUDICIAL SYSTEM AND RACISM AGAINST PEOPLE OF AFRICAN DESCENT: THE CASES OF BRAZIL, COLOMBIA, THE DOMINICAN REPUBLIC AND PERU (2004).

Kadi v. Israel Railways, (Isr.) http://employment.molsa.gov.il/English/NewsRoom/PressReleases/Pages/EEOCCommissionerEnd8YearTerm.aspx.

KAMEL, ALI. NAO SOMOS RACISTAS: UMA REACAO AOS QUE QUEREM NOS TRANSFORMAR NUMA NACAO BICOLOR, (Sao Paulo: Nova Fronteira, 2006).

Kapai, Puja, *Status of Ethnic Minorities in Hong-Kong 1997–2014: The Rights of Ethnic Minorities Under The Law: Equality And Non-Discrimination*, UNIV. OF HONG-KONG: CENT. FOR COMP. & PUB. LAW (2015).

KHAITAN, TARUNABH. A THEORY OF DISCRIMINATION LAW (2015).

Koshan, Jennifer & Jonnette Watson Hamilton, *The Continual Reinvention of Section 15 of the Charter*, 64 UNIV. NEW BRUNSWICK L.J. 19 (2013).

La Razon, *Suspenden A Unos 10 Maestros Por Discriminacion*, LA RAZON: SOCIEDAD (Mar. 22, 2018), http://www.la-razon.com/sociedad/Suspenden-maestros-discriminacion_0_2896510324.html.

Law Against Racism and All Forms of Discrimination (Law 045) (Bolivia).

Lee, Christina, *Toward a Transformative Equality: A Comparison of South Africa's and the United States' Constitutional Equality Doctrines*, 16 SCHOLAR: ST. MARY'S L. REV. & SOC. JUST. 749 (2014).

Lei n.º 134/99, Diário da República—I Série-A, 5945 (1999) (Portugal) https://dre.pt/application/file/a/532477.

Lei n.º 18/2004, Diário da República—I Série-A, Artigo 2º [Article 2], 2971 (2004) (Portugal) https://dre.pt/application/dir/pdfisdip/2004/05/110A00/29712974.pdf.

Lei n.º 27/2005, Diário da República—I Série-A, Artigo 2º [Article 2], 874 (2005) (Portugal) https://dre.pt/application/conteudo/618939.

Lei n.º 7/2009, Diário da República—1.ª série-N.º 30, 933 (2009) (Portugal) https://dre.pt/application/dir/pdfisdip/2009/02/03000/0092601029.pdf (this provision pertains to Article 24 of the Labor Code, contained in the Annex of Lei n.º 7/2009).

Lei No. 10.639/2003 (Braz.).

Lei No. 12.711/2012 (Braz.).

Lei No. 7.347, de 24 Julho 1985 (Braz.).

Lei No. 7.347, de 24 Julho 1985, D.O.U. of 25 Julho 1985, as amended by Law Nos. 8.078 of September 11, 1990; 8.884 de June 11, 1994; 9.494 de September 10, 1997 (Braz.); Provisional Measure No. 2.102–28 de February 23, 2001 (Braz.).

Ley No. 115 de Febrero 8 de 1994, Art. 160, §10 (Colom.).

Ley No. 24-97 (Dominican Republic).

Ley No. 24-97, Párrafo III, Art. 9 (Dominican Republic), http://www.iin.oea.org/badaj/docs/l24-97do.htm#Texto (modifies prior articulos 336, 337 and 339).

Ley No. 641, 13 Nov. 2007, Código Penal [Criminal Code] art. 36.5, La Gaceta, Diario Oficial [L.G.], 4 July 2018 (Nicar.).

Ley No. 641, Criminal Code, Art. 427, 428 (Nicar.).

Ley No. 70 de Agosto 27 de 1993, Art. 7 (Colom.).

Lino, Dylan. *Thinking Outside the Constitution on Indigenous Constitutional Recognition: Entrenching the Racial Discrimination Act*, 91 Austl. L.J. 381 (2017).

Litvinoff, Saul. *Moral Damages*, 38 La. L. Rev. 1 (1977).

Lugones, Maria C. & Elizabeth V. Spelman, *Have We Got A Theory For You! Feminist Theory, Cultural Imperialism And The Demand For The 'Woman's Voice'*, 6 WOMEN'S STUD. INT'L F. 573, 573–581 (1983); ELIZABETH V. SPELMAN, INESSENTIAL WOMAN: PROBLEMS OF EXCLUSION IN FEMINIST THOUGHT (1988).

Machado, Marta Rodriguez de Assis et al., *Racismo e Insulto Racial na Sociedade Brasileira: Dinâmicas de reconhecimento e invizibilização a partir do direito*, 35.03 Novos Estud. 11 (2016).

MACKINNON, CATHARINE A. BUTTERFLY POLITICS (2017).

MacKinnon, Catherine A. *Substantive Equality: A Perspective*, 94 MINN. L. REV. 1, 1–27, 10 (2011).

Maeso, Silvia Rodríguez. *'Civilising' the Roma/Gypsies. Public policies, 'employability' and the depoliticisation of (anti-'employability' and the depoliticisation of (anti-) racism in* Portugal, 22 IDENTITIES GLOBAL STUD. CULTURE POWER 53 (2014).

MAKING EQUALITY COUNT: IRISH AND INTERNATIONAL RESEARCH MEASURING EQUALITY AND DISCRIMINATION (Laurence Bond, Frances McGinnity & Helen Russell eds., 2010).

McDonnell Douglas Corp., v. Green, 411 U.S. 792 (1973).

Meredith v. Jefferson County Board of Education, 548 U.S. 938 (2006).

Michael Arce Mendez v. Fernando Encaláda Parrales, Proceso No. 17124-2014-0585 (Ecuador).

Michelman, Frank J. *Reasonable Umbrage: Race and Constitutional Antidiscrimination Law in the United States and South Africa*, 117 HARV. L. REV. 1378 (2004).

MINISTERIO DE CULTURAS Y TURISMO: VICEMINISTERIO DE DESCOLONIZACION, *Direccion General de Lucha Contra el Racismo, Reporte Estadistico de Denuncias por Racismo y/o Discriminacion Hasta el 31 de Diciembre de 2017*, (2017), http://noracismo.gob.bo/archivos-pdf/REPORTE-DENUNCIAS-AL-31-DICIEMBRE-2017.pdf.

Mitchell, Michael J. & Charles H. Wood, *Ironies of Citizenship: Skin Color, Police Brutality, and the Challenge to Democracy in Brazil*, 77 SOCIAL FORCES 1001–20 (1999).

MÖSCHEL, MATHIAS. LAW, LAWYERS AND RACE: CRITICAL RACE THEORY FROM THE US TO EUROPE (2014).

Mundlak, Guy. *The Law of Equal Opportunities in Employment: Between Equality and Polarization*, 30 COMP. LAB. L. & POL'Y J. 213 (2009).

[National Human Rights Commission Act], Act No. 6481, May 24, 2001, *amended by* Act. No. 11413, Mar. 21, 2012, ch. 1 art. 2, (S. Kor.) (http://elaw.klri.re.kr/eng_service/lawView.do?hseq=37724&lang=ENG).

[Nationality Act], Act. No. 8892, Mar. 14, 2008, *amended by* Act. No. 12421, Mar. 18, 2014, art. 5, (S. Kor.) (http://elaw.klri.re.kr/eng_service/lawView.do?hseq=32444&lang=ENG).

Neves, Céu. *Comissão contra a discriminação racial atua desde 2005 e apenas conseguiu sete condenações*, DIARIO DE NOTICIAS (Mar. 22, 2012), https://advance.lexis.com/api/permalink/9f08b576-3086-4e29-b491-5cbfb299e4f5/?context=1000516.

NIHONKOKU KENPŌ [KENPŌ] [CONSTITUTION], art. 14, para. 1 (JAPAN).

Oboler, Suzanne, *The Foreignness of Racism: Pride and Prejudice among Peru's Limenos in the 1990s*, *in* NEITHER ENEMIES NOR FRIENDS 75, 75–100 (Anani Dzidzienyo & Suzanne Oboler eds., 2005).

Padilla, Laura. *Intersectionality and Positionality: Situating Women of Color in the Affirmative Action Dialogue*, 66 FORDHAM L. REV. 843, 843–929.

Parents Involved in Community Schools v. Seattle School District No. 1, 551 U.S. 701 (2007).

Pedrosa et al., Renato H.L., "Academic Performance, Students' Background and Affirmative Action at a Brazilian University," *Higher Education Management and Policy* 19 (2007), (1–20).

Personnel Administrator of Massachusetts v. Feeney, 442 U.S. 256 (1979).

Petersen, Carole J. & Kelley Loper, *Equal Opportunities Law Reform in Hong Kong: The Impact of International Norms and Civil Society Advocacy*, *in* REFORMING LAW REFORM: PERSPECTIVES FROM HONG KONG AND BEYOND 173 (Michael Tilbury, Simon N.M. Young & Ludwig Ng eds., 2014).

Pinheiro, Paulo Sergio. *The Rule of Law and the Underprivileged in Latin America: Introduction, in* THE (UN)RULE OF LAW AND THE UNDERPRIVILEGED IN LATIN AMERICA (Juan E. Mendez, Guillermo O'Donnell & Paulo Sergio Pinheiro eds., 1999).

Porter, Bruce, *Twenty Years of Equality Rights: Reclaiming Expectations*, 23 WINDSOR Y.B. ACCESS JUST. 145 (2005).

President of the Republic of South Africa and Another v. Hugo 1997 (6) BCLR 708 (CC) (S. Afr.).

Qedar, Yair, *Sharing experience to bring equal opportunities*, ENPI Info Centre, Feature no. 31 (2010), www.enpi-info.eu.

Race Discrimination Ordinance, (2009) Cap. 602 (H.K.), *available at* https://www.elegislation.gov.hk/hk/cap602 (last visited Aug. 29, 2018) (Hong Kong).

RACE, POLITICS, AND EDUCATION IN BRAZIL: AFFIRMATIVE ACTION IN HIGHER EDUCATION (Rosana Heringer, Ollie Johnson & Ollie A. Johnson, III eds., 2015).

Racusen, Seth, A Mulato Cannot Be Prejudiced: The Legal Construction of Racial Discrimination in Contemporary Brazil, 87–8 (2002) (unpublished Ph.D. dissertation, Massachusetts Institute of Technology).

Racusen, Seth, *"Making the 'Impossible' Determination: Flexible Identity and Targeted Opportunity in Contemporary Brazil*, 36 CONN. L. REV. 787, 787–829 (2004).

Racusen, Seth, *Fictions of Identity and Brazilian Affirmative Action*, 21 NAT'L BLACK L.J. 1 (2009); "Cotas No Brasil: Um Panorama do Aplicação de Políticas Afirmativas Nas Universidades Públicas," Revista Adusp 43 (July 2008), 6–39.

Reed, Jean-Pierre, *Theorist of Subaltern Subjectivity: Antonio Gramsci, Popular Beliefs, Political Passion, and Reciprocal Learning, Critical Sociology*, 39 CRITICAL SOCIOLOGY Issue 4, 561 561–91 (2012).

Ricci v. DeStefano, 557 U.S. 557 (2009).

Rice, Simon & Tim Soutphommasane, *The Racial Discrimination Act at 40*, 89 AUSTL. L.J. 303, 304 (2015).

Rodríguez-Garavito, César, *En Defensa de las Acciones Afirmativas*, EL ESPECTADOR (July 13, 2009), http://www.elespectador.com/columna150499-defensa-de-acciones-afirmativas.

Rojas, Hugo. *Legal Responses to Discriminatory Actions: A Comparative Analysis*, 5 LOY. U. CHI. INT'L L. REV. 127 (2008).

S. AFR. CONST., 1996 § 8(2).

S. AFR. CONST., 1996 § 9.

Sanders, Edmund. *New Israeli Laws Will Increase Discrimination Against Arabs, Critics Say*, L.A. TIMES, Mar. 24, 2011.

SANTOS, BOAVENTURA DE SOUSA SANTOS. TOWARD A NEW LEGAL COMMON SENSE 458–493 (William Twining & Christopher McCrudden eds., 2nd ed. 2002).

Scales-Trent, Judy. *Black Women and the Constitution: Finding Our Place, Asserting Our Rights*, 24 HARV. C.R.-C.L. L. REV. 9 (1989).

Scarborough, Cathy. Note, *Conceptualizing Black Women's Employment Experiences*, 98 YALE L.J. 1457 (1989).

Schuette v. Coalition to Defend Affirmative Action, 572 U.S. 291 (2014).

Schwartz, Hart. *Making Sense of Section 15 of the Charter*, 29 N'ATL J. CONST. L. 201 (2011).

Selmi, Michael. *Theorizing Systemic Disparate Treatment Law: After Wal-Mart v. Dukes*, 32 BERKELEY J. EMP. & LAB. L. 477 (2011).

Sentencia No. 479-2015-2JPL-PJ-CSJJU (Peru).

Smith v. City of Jackson, 351 F.3d 183 (5th Cir. 2003).

SOLANKE, IYIOLA, DISCRIMINATION AS STIGMA: A THEORY OF ANTI-DISCRIMINATION LAW (2017).

Soutphommasane, Tim. *Forty Years of the Racial Discrimination Act*, 40 ALTERNATIVE L.J. 153 (2015).

SPELMAN, ELIZABETH V. INESSENTIAL WOMAN: PROBLEMS OF EXCLUSION IN FEMINIST THOUGHT (1988).

Spivak, Gayatri Chakravorty. *Can the Subaltern Speak?*, *in* MARXISM AND THE INTERPRETATION OF CULTURE 271, 271–313 (Cary Nelson & Lawrence Grossberg eds., 1988).

St. Mary's Honor Center v. Hicks, 509 U.S. 502 (1993).

"STF declared the constitutionality of the quota system at the University of Brasilia," STF Internacional (Federal Supreme Court of Brazil news portal), April 26, 2012, http://www2.stf.jus.br/portalStfInternacional/cms/destaquesClipping.php?sigla=portalStfDestaque_en_us&idConteudo=207138.

Sternlight, Jean R. *In Search of the Best Procedure for Enforcing Employment Discrimination Laws: A Comparative Analysis*, 78 TULANE L. REV. 1401 (2004).

Suk, Julie C., *Quotas and Consequences: A Transnational Re-evaluation*, *in* PHILOSOPHICAL FOUNDATIONS OF DISCRIMINATION LAW (Deborah Hellman & Sophia Moreau, eds., 2013).

Suk, Julie Chi-hye. *Equal by Comparison: Unsettling Assumptions of Antidiscrimination Law*, 55 AM. J. COMP. L. 295 (2007).

"Supremo declara constitucionalidade do ProUni," Secretaria de Políticas de Promoção da Igualdade Racial, Últimas Notícias, May 4, 2012, http://www.seppir.gov.br/noticias/ultimas_noticias/2012/05/supremo-declara-constitucionalidade-do-prouni.

T.J.R.J., Embargos Infringentes No. 2005.005.00060 (Braz.).

Tamir, Michal. *The Freedom to Exclude: The Case of Israeli Society*, 49 ISR. L. REV. 237 (2016).

Texas. Department of Housing and Community Affairs v. The Inclusive Communities Project, Inc., 135 S. Ct. 2507 (2015).

Thackrah, Andrew, *From Neutral to Drive—Australian Anti-Discrimination Law and Identity*, 33 ALTERNATIVE L.J. 31 (2008).

THE AFFIRMATIVE ACTION DEBATE (George E. Curry ed., 1996).

[The Nationality Law], Law No. 147 of 1950, as amended by Law No. 268 of 1952, Law No. 45 of 1984, Law No. 89 of 1993 and Law. No. 147 of 2004, Law No. 88 of 2008n (Japan) (http://www.moj.go.jp/ENGLISH/information/tnl-01.html).

THE NUREMBERG LAWS: INSTITUTIONALIZED ANTI-SEMITISM (Amy Newman ed., 1999).

The Promotion of Equality and Prevention of Unfair Discrimination Act of 2000, Equality Act 4 of 2000 (S. Afr.).

Vargas, Jorge A. *Moral Damages*, 38 LA. L. REV. 1, 1–28 (1977).

Vargas, Jorge A. *Moral Damages Under the Civil Law of Mexico: Are These Damages Equivalent to U.S. Punitive Damages?*, 35 UNIV. MIAMI INTER-AMERICAN L. REV. 193 (2004).

Vega Sfrani, Gonzalo. *Universidad Reserva La Mitad de sus Cupos Para Negros y Desata Polemica*, EL MERCUIRO, (Oct. 22, 2006), http://www.ifcs.ufrj.br/~observa/noticias/elmercurio/discriminacion_22.htm.

Village of Arlington Heights v. Metropolitan Housing Development Corp., 429 U.S. 252 (1977).

Wards Cove Packing Co. v. Atonio, 490 U.S. 642 (1989).

Watson v. Fort Worth Bank & Trust, 487 U.S. 977 (1988).

White v. Washington Public Power Supply System, 692 F.2d 1286 (9th Cir. 1982).

Williams, Michelle Y. *African Nova Scotian Restorative Justice: A Change Has Gotta Come*, 36 DALHOUSIE L.J. 419 (2013).

Williamson v. A.G. Edwards & Sons, Inc., 876 F.2d 69 (8th Cir. 1989).

Yi, Yujin. *The Status Quo of Racial Discrimination in Japan and the Republic of Korea, and the Need to Provide for Anti-Discrimination Laws*, 7 COLUM. J. RACE L. 410 (2017).

Zabala, Joaquín Robles. *Una Enfermedad Incurable*, REVISTA SEMANA (Dec. 15, 2014), https://www.semana.com/opinion/articulo/una-enfermedad-incurable-opinion-joaquin-robles-zabala/412321-3.

ZWEIGERT, KONRAD & HEIN KÖTZ, AN INTRODUCTION TO COMPARATIVE LAW (Tony Weir trans., Oxford University Press 1998) (1977).

www.ingramcontent.com/pod-product-compliance
Lightning Source LLC
Chambersburg PA
CBHW031333230926
51848CB00001B/222
9789004345942